BILLIARDS

THE OFFICIAL RULES & RECORDS BOOK

1993

**BILLIARD CONGRESS
OF AMERICA**

BCA RULES COMMITTEE
Jerry Briesath Chairman; Gary Benson, Jeff Carter, Randy Goettlicher,
Bob Hunter, Peg Ledman, John Lewis, Richard Rhorer

BCA STATISTICS/RECORDS COMMITTEE
Michael Shamos Chairman; Robert Byrne, Charles Ursitti

Published By
BILLIARD CONGRESS OF AMERICA
1700 S. 1st. Ave.
Iowa City, Iowa 52240
(319) 351-2112
FAX: (319) 351-7767

ISBN 1-878493-03-5
ISSN 1047-244

FOREWORD

The Billiard Congress of America came into existence in 1948 along with the now defunct National Billiard Council. From its beginning, BCA has attempted to unify our industry; bringing together player, proprietor, retailer and manufacturer. The rules contained in this book were established with this goal in mind: facilitating a better understanding of billiards.

We wish to recognize the Rules Committee, noted on the previous page, for their dedication and contribution to this effort.

Mission Statement of the Billiard Congress of America

The mission of the BCA is to govern and promote the sport of billiards (pocket, carom and snooker) in the United States and world-wide by establishing rules and equipment specifications, promoting and sanctioning amateur and professional tournaments and helping to increase awareness of and participation in the sport to all people, while working with all integers to increase the overall growth of billiards. BCA will perform all of its functions on a non-profit basis with the highest ethical standards and fair treatment of all of its members and the entire billiards community.

RECOGNITION OF CONTRIBUTIONS

The BCA would like to especially thank the following individuals and organizations for their invaluable contributions to the 1993 Official Rules and Records Book:

George Aronek
Gary Benson
Jerry Briesath
Robert Byrne
Craig Connelly
Jeff Carter
Pat Fleming
Randy Goettlicher
Richard Grimaldi

Bobby Hunter
Billy Incardona
Robert Kervick
Peg Ledman
Richard Rhorer
Eddy Schotborgh
Michael Shamos
Terry Smith
Mike Weaver

Pot Black Magazine
Professional Billiard Tour Association
United States Billiard Association
United States Snooker Association
Women's Professional Billiard Association
World Pool-Billiard Association
World Professional Billiard and Snooker Association

THE STATE OF WORLD RULES - 1993

Cue Sports have exploded worldwide! Organizing the expansion in the numbers of people playing, and standardizing the formats and rules being used for the greater amount of competitions have become a necessary and responsible challenge.

The World Confederation of Billiard Sports delivered the first-ever official application for recognition of cue sports to the International Olympic Committee in Lausanne, Switzerland, in September, 1992. The WCBS recognizes the three cue disciplines of pool, carom and snooker as suitably organized worldwide, and the world organizations it recognizes are the World Pool-Billiard Association (pool), the Union Mondiale de Billard (carom) and the World Snooker Federation (snooker).

The Billiard Congress of America has taken great care to include the internationally standardized rules for 3-cushion billiards (see USBA rules) and snooker (see International Snooker rules) in the 1993 edition of this book.

In addition the BCA (representing the various federations of North America) has worked in cooperation with the other confederations of WPA-the European Pocket Billiard Federation (representing 17 national federations), the Asian Pocket Billiard Union (representing 7 national federations), and the Australasian Pool Association (representing 2 national federations) to produce the first-ever world standardized rules for the major tournament games of Nine Ball and 14.1 Continuous. These rules, as detailed in the 1993 edition of the BCA Rules and Records Book, are the same rules in current use by both the Women's Professional Billiard Association and the Professional Billiard Tour Association in the United States.

-John Lewis
Editor

TABLE OF CONTENTS

MAJOR AMENDMENTS IN THE 1993 BCA RULES AND RECORDS BOOK

- The "History" section has been updated and expanded.

- In the "Equipment Specifications" section, the "Table Bed Height" has been refined. The "Pocket Openings" section has been researched thoroughly, and now includes specifications for mouth, throat, shelf and drop point slate radius.

- The rules for both "Baseball Pocket Billiards" and "Poker Pocket Billiards" have been reintroduced to the book by popular demand.

- The entire "Tournament Results and Records" section has been updated in all categories, with a special emphasis on expanding the 3-Cushion Billiards records and listing snooker champions.

TOURNAMENT RULES

- In accordance with the standardized rules of the World Pool-Billiard Association, touching any ball during a match which is refereed is a foul. In a match which is not refereed, the rules for "cue ball fouls only" will be utilized according to the speific game.

GENERAL RULES

- To conform with the rules of carom billiards, snooker and the tradition of all cue sports, any object ball that jumps off the table in any game of pocket billiards is now ruled to be a foul, with the penalty explained in the rules of each spcific games.

- To conform with the rules of carom and snooker, any ball that jumps the table, contacts any "non-permanent" fixture of equipment of the table (such as a piece of chalk, the overhead table light, etc.), and returns to the bed of the table is ruled a foul.

- A more specific guideline for judging the legality of "double hits" is defined.

EIGHT BALL

- Any object balls pocked on a scratch or illegal hit remain pocketed, regardless of whether the table is a coin-op or non coin-op table.

NINE BALL

- The 1993 rules reflect the now commonly used "express" rules which have been adopted by the professional player associations and the World Pool-Billiard Association.

14.1 CONTINUOUS

- The 1993 rules reflect a return to the traditional penalty for a player committing three consecutive fouls: the loss of 15 pionts with the balls being reracked, and the offending player breaking according to the requirements of the opening break. Both professional player associations favor this rule, and the text of the BCA 14.1 rules corresponds exactly with those of the World Pool-Billiard Association.

A Brief History of the Noble Game of Billiards

by Mike Shamos

The history of billiards is long and very rich. The game has been played by kings and commoners, presidents, mental patients, ladies, gentlemen, and hustlers alike. It evolved from a lawn game similar to the croquet played sometime during the 15th century in Northern Europe and probably in France. Play was moved indoors to a wooden table with green cloth to simulate grass, and a simple border was placed around the edges. The balls were shoved, rather than struck, with wooden sticks called "maces." The term "billiard" is derived from French, either from the word "billart," one of the wooden sticks, of "bille," a ball.

The game was originally played with two balls on a six-pocket table with a hoop similar to a croquet wicket and an upright stick used as a target. During the eighteenth century, the hoop and target gradually disappeared, leaving only the balls and pockets. Most of our information about early billiards comes from accounts of playing by royalty and other nobles. It has been known as the "Noble Game of Billiards" since the early 1800's, but there is evidence that people from all walks of life have played the game since its inception. In 1600, the game was familiar enough to the public that Shakespeare mentioned it in Antony and Cleopatra. Seventy-five years later, the first book of billiard rules remarked of England that there were "few Towns of note therein which hath not a publick Billiard-Table."

The cue stick was developed in the late 1600's. When the ball lay near a rail, the mace was very inconvenient to use because of its large head. In such a case, the players would turn the mace around and use its handle to strike the ball. The handle was called a "queue"–meaning "tail"–from which we get the word "cue." For a long time only men were allowed to use the cue; women were forced to use the mace because it was felt they were more likely to rip the cloth with the sharper cue.

Tables originally had flat vertical walls for rails and their only function was to keep the balls from falling off. They resembled river banks and even used to be called "banks." Players discovered that balls could bounce off the rails and began deliberately aiming at them. Thus a "bank shot" is one in which a ball is made to rebound from a cushion as part of the shot.

Billiard equipment improved rapidly in England after 1800, largely because of the Industrial Revolution. Chalk was used to increase friction between the ball and the cue stick even before cues had tips. The leather cue tip, with which a player can apply side-spin to the ball, was perfected by 1823. Visitors from England showed Americans how to use spin which explains why it is called "English" in the United States but nowhere else. (The British themselves refer

1

to it as "side.") The two-piece cue arrived in 1829. Slate became popular as a material for table beds around 1835. Goodyear discovered vulcanization of rubber in 1839 and by 1845 it was used to make billiard cushions. By 1850 the billiard table had essentially evolved into its current form.

The dominant billiard game in Britain from about 1770 until the 1920's was English Billiards, played with three balls and six pockets on a large rectangular table. A two-to-one ratio of length to width became standard in the 18th century. Before then, there were no fixed table dimensions. The British billiard tradition is carried on today primarily through the game of Snooker, a complex and colorful game combining offensive and defensive aspects and played on the same equipment as English Billiards but with 22 balls instead of three. The British appetite for Snooker is approached only by the American passion for baseball; it is possible to see Snooker competition every day in Britain.

Billiards In The United States

How billiards came to America has not been positively established. There are tales that it was brought to St. Augustine by the Spaniards in the 1580's but research has failed to reveal any trace of the game there. More likely it was brought over by Dutch and English settlers. A number of American cabinetmakers in the 1700's turned out exquisite billiard tables, although in small quantities. Nevertheless, the game did spread throughout the Colonies. Even George Washington was reported to have won a match in 1748. By 1830, despite primitive equipment, public rooms devoted entirely to billiards appeared. The most famous of them was Bassford's, a New York room that catered to stockbrokers. Here a number of American versions of billiards were developed, including Pin Pool, played with small wooden targets like miniature bowling pins, and Fifteen-Ball Pool, described later.

The American billiard industry and the incredible rise in popularity of the game are due to Michael Phelan, the father of American billiards. Phelan emigrated from Ireland and in 1850 wrote the first American book on the game. He was influential in devising rules and setting standards of behavior. An inventor, he added diamonds to the table to assist in aiming, and developed new table and cushion designs. He was also the first American billiard columnist. On January 1, 1859, the first of his weekly articles appeared in Leslie's Illustrated Weekly. A few months later, Phelan won a prize of $15,000 at Detroit in the first important stake match held in the United States. He was a tireless promoter of the game and created the manufacturing company of Phelan and Collender. In 1884 the company merged with its chief competitor, J.M. Brunswick & Balke, to form the Brunswick-Balke-Collender Company, which tightly controlled all aspects of the game until the 1950's. Its successor, Brunswick Billiards, is still the largest American manufacturer.

The dominant American billiard game until the 1870's was American Four-Ball Billiards, usually played on a large (11 or 12-foot), four-pocket table with four balls–two white and red. It was a direct extension of English Billiards. Points were scored by pocketing balls, scratching the cue ball, or by making caroms on two or three balls. A "carom" is the act of hitting two object balls with the cue ball at one stroke. With so many balls, there were many different ways of scoring and it was possible to make up to 13 points on a single shot. American Four-Ball produced two offspring, both of which surpassed it in popularity by the late 1870's. One, simple caroms played with three balls on a pocketless table, is sometimes known as "Straight Rail," the forerunner of all carom games. The other popular game was American Fifteen-Ball Pool, the predecessor of modern pocket billiards. The word "pool" means a collective bet, or ante. Many non-billiard games, such as poker, involve a pool but it was to pocket billiards that the name became attached. The term "poolroom" now means a place where pool is played, but in the 19th century a poolroom was a betting parlor for horse racing. Pool tables were installed so patrons could pass the time between races. The two became connected in the public mind, but the unsavory connotation of "pool-room" came from the betting that took place there, not from billiards.

Fifteen-Ball Pool was played with 15 object balls, numbered 1 through 15. For sinking a ball, the player received a number of points equal to the value of the ball. The sum of the ball values in a rack is 120, so the first player who received more than half the total, or 61, was the winner. This game, also called "61-Pool," was used in the first American championship pool tournament held in 1878 and won by Cyrille Dion, a Canadian. In 1888, it was thought more fair to count the number of balls pocketed by a player and not their numerical value. Thus Continuous Pool replaced Fifteen-Ball Pool as the championship game. The player who sank the last ball of a rack would break the next rack and his point total would be kept "continuously" from one rack to the next.

Eight-Ball was invented shortly after 1900; Straight Pool followed in 1910. Nine-Ball seems to have developed around 1920. One-Pocket has ancestors that are older than any of these; the idea of the game was described in 1775 and complete rules for a British form appeared in 1869.

From 1878 until 1956, pool and billiard championship tournaments were held almost annually, with one-on-one challenge matches filling the remaining months. At times, including during the Civil War, billiard results received wider coverage that war news. Players were so renowned that cigarette cards were issued featuring them. The BCA Hall of Fame honors many players from this era, including Jacob Schaefer, Sr. and his son, Jake Jr., Frank Taberski, Alfredo De Oro, and Johnny Layton. The first half of this century was the era of the billiard personality. In 1906 Willie Hoppe, 18, established the world supremacy of American players by beating Maurice Vignaux of France at balkline. Balkline is a version of carom billiards with lines drawn on the table to form rectangles. When both object balls lie in the same rectangle, the number of shots that can be made is restricted. This makes the game much harder because the player must cause one of the balls to leave the rectangle, and hopefully return. When balkline lost its popularity during the 1930's, Hoppe began a new career in three-cushion billiards which he dominated until his retirement in 1952. Hoppe was a true American legend–a boy of humble roots whose talent was discovered early, a world champion as a teenager, and a gentleman who held professional titles for almost 50 years. One newspaper reported that under his manipulation, the balls moved "as if under a magic spell." To many fans, billiards meant Hoppe.

While the term "billiards" refers to all games played on billiard tables, with or without pockets, some people take billiards to mean carom games only and use pool for pocket games. Carom games, particularly balkline, dominated public attention until 1919, when Ralph Greenleaf's pool playing captured the nation's attention. For the next 20 years he gave up the title on only a few occasions. Through the 1930's, both pool and billiards, particularly three-cushion billiards, shared the spotlight. In 1941 the Mosconi era began and carom games declined in importance. Pool went to war several times as a popular recreation for the troops. Professional players toured military posts giving exhibitions; some even worked in the defense industry. But the game had more trouble emerging from World War II than it had getting into it. Returning soldiers were in a mood to buy houses and build careers, and the charm of an afternoon spent at the pool table was a thing of the past. Room after room closed quietly and by the end of the 1950's it looked as though the game might pass into oblivion. Willie Mosconi, who won or successfully defended the pocket billiard title 19 times, retired as champion in 1956.

Billiards was revived by two electrifying events, one in 1961, the other in 1986. The first was the release of the movie, The Hustler, based on the novel by Walter Tevis. The black-and-white film depicted the dark life of a pool hustler with Paul Newman in the title role. The sound of clicking balls sent America into a billiard frenzy. New rooms opened all over the country and for the remainder of the 60's pool flourished until social concerns, the Vietnam War, and a desire for outdoor coeducational activities led to a decline in billiard interest. By 1985, there were only two public rooms left in Manhattan, down from several thousand during the 1930's. In 1986, The Color of Money, a sequel to The Hustler with Paul Newman in the same role and Tom Cruise as a an up-and-coming professional, brought the excitement of pool to a new generation. The result was the opening of "upscale" rooms catering to people whose senses would have been offended by the old rooms if they had ever seen them. This trend began slowly in 1987 and has since surged, even resulting in a public stock offering in 1991 by Jillian's, a Boston-based room chain.

While the game has had its heroes since the early 1800's, it has had to wage a constant battle for respectability. Poolrooms were often the target of politicians and legislators eager to show an ability to purge immorality from the community. Even today, obtaining a billiard license can require compliance with antiquated regulations. In the 1920's, the poolroom was an environment in which men gathered to loiter, smoke, fight, bet, and play. The rooms of the 1990's bear no resemblance to those of earlier times. The new rooms have a cachet approaching that of chic restaurants and night clubs. They offer quality equipment, expert instruction, and the chance for people to meet socially for a friendly evening. Being totally without stigma, these rooms are responsible for introducing an entire new audience to the game and are resulting in the greatest surge in billiard interest in the United States in over a century.

Women In Billiards

Until very recently, billiards was completely dominated by men. The atmosphere of the poolroom was very forbidding and a woman would have had trouble being accepted there. Nonetheless, women have been enthusiastic players since the game was brought up from the ground in the 15th century. For over two hundred years women of fashion have played. Since the 1890's, there has always been at least one prominent female professional on the scene, from May Kaarlus, a spectacular turn-of-the-century trick-shot artist, to Ruth McGinnis, who toured with Willie Mosconi in the 1930's and could beat most men, to Dorothy Wise, winner of the first five U.S. Open tournaments for women, and Jean Balukas, who took the next seven. Today there are enough women professionals to merit a separate organization, the WPBA, to solicit commercial sponsorship and organize tournaments. It is very difficult for a woman to develop billiard skill because male players, her family, and friends usually do not support her efforts and it is not easy to find experienced women instructors or coaches. As this situation changes, we can expect women to equal men in ability and take the game to even greater heights.

–Mike Shamos is Curator of *The Billiard Archive*,
a nonprofit organization set up
to preserve the game's history.

BCA EQUIPMENT SPECIFICATIONS

TABLE SIZES:
Pocket Billiard Tables ....4 by 8 and 4 $\frac{1}{2}$ by 9
Carom Billiard Tables .... 4 $\frac{1}{2}$ by 9 and 5 by 10
American Snooker Tables ....4 $\frac{1}{2}$ by 9 and 5 by 10

PLAYING AREA:
Measured from the cloth covered nose of cushion rubber to the opposite cushion rubber, both width and length:
4 by 8 table ....playing area 44" width by 88" length
4 by 8 table............................. playing area of 46" width by 92" length
4 $\frac{1}{2}$ by 9 table .... playing area of 50" width by 100" length
5 by 10 table .... playing area of 56" width by 112" length
BCA will sanction Tournament Play on Home and Coin-operated tables produced in sizes other than those recognized above, if the playing area width is one-half the length, measured cushion to opposite cushion.

TABLE BED HEIGHT:
The table bed playing surface, when measured from the bottom of the table leg, will be 29 $\frac{1}{4}$" minimum to 30 $\frac{1}{4}$" maximum

POCKET OPENINGS AND MEASUREMENTS:
Pocket billiard tables: pocket openings are measured at two points - the first being measured between opposing cushion noses where the direction changes into the pocket (tip to tip). This is called the **mouth**. The second point of measurement is at the narrowest point at the back of the facing. This is called the **throat**.

Corner Pocket: Mouth ....4 $\frac{7}{8}$" minimum to 5 $\frac{1}{8}$" maximum
                      Throat ....4" minimum to 4 $\frac{1}{4}$" maximum

Side Pocket: Mouth ....5 $\frac{3}{8}$" minimum to 5 $\frac{5}{8}$" maximum
                      Throat ....4 $\frac{3}{8}$" minimum to 4 $\frac{7}{8}$" maximum

Vertical Pocket Angle   12±1 degree

Shelf: The shelf is measured from the center of the imaginary line that goes from one side of the mouth to the other where the nose of the cushion changes direction to the center of the vertical cut of the slate pocket radius.

Shelf: Corner Pocket ....1 $\frac{5}{8}$" minimum to 1 $\frac{7}{8}$" maximum
                  Side Pocket ....0" minimum to $\frac{3}{8}$" maximum

Drop Point Slate Radius: The pocket radius measured from the vertical cut of the slate to the playing surface.

Drop Point Slate Radius .... $^1/_8$" r. minimum to $^1/_4$" r. maximum

PLAYING BED:

The playing surface must be capable, either by its own strength or a combination of its strength and that of the table baseframe, of maintaining an overall flatness within ± .020" lengthwise and .010" across the width. Further, this surface should have an additional deflection not to exceed .030" when loaded with a concentrated static force of 200 pounds at its center. If more than one slab is employed, the slab joints must be in the same plane within .005" after leveling and shimming. The bed must be covered with a billiard fabric, the major portion of which is made of wool, with proper tension to avoid unwanted ball roll-off. Commercial tables must have a 1"-3 piece set of slate with a wooden frame minimum $^3/_4$" attached to slate. All playing surfaces must be secured to base frame with screws or bolts.

CUSHION:

Rubber cushions should be triangular in shape and molded with the conventional K-66 profile with a base of 1 $^3/_{16}$" and a nose height of 1", with control fabric molded to the top and base area of the cushion. On carom billiard tables, the triangular K-55 profile cushion is to be maintained, with the control fabric on the underside of the cushion to effect a slower rebound action. On snooker tables, the triangular K66 profile or L-shaped snooker cushion is to be used. The balance of the rail section to which the rubber cushion is glued should be of hardwood construction and attached to the slate bed with a minimum of three (3) heavy duty, threaded rail bolts per rail.

BILLIARD BALLS:

Molded and finished in a perfect sphere, with both dynamic and static balance, in the following weights and diameters as used in the following games:

Pocket Billiard Balls
  Weight: 5 $^1/_2$ to 6 oz. .... *Diameter: 2$^1/_4$"

Carom Balls
  Weight: 7 to 7 $^1/_2$ oz. .... *Diameter: 2$^{27}/_{64}$"
                                                                                             2$^3/_8$"
                                                                                             2$^7/_{16}$"

Snooker Balls
  Weight: 5 to 5 $^1/_2$ oz. .... *Diameter: 2$^1/_8$"
                                                                                             2$^1/_{16}$"
*Diameter tolerance of (plus or minus) .005"

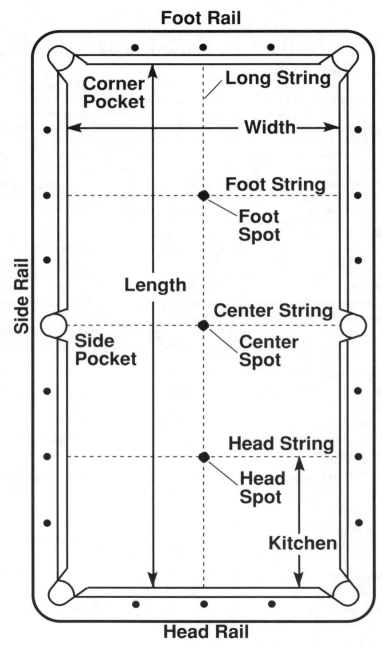

Diagram 1

GLOSSARY OF BILLIARD TERMS

The following glossary contains those billiard terms and definitions essential to utilization of the rules of games provided in this book. In addition to definitions of such terms, there are also many references to equipment, accessories and phrases in common usage by billiard players.

Each definition begins with the term in bold face type, followed by a parenthetical notation of the game variation or classification in which the term is used or to which it primarily applies.

Where a diagram or other supplemental information is available elsewhere in this book, it is referenced parenthetically following the definition.

ANGLED. (Snooker, pocket games) When the corner of a pocket prevents a player shooting the cue ball directly at an object ball. (See *corner-hooked*.)

ANGLE SHOT. (Pocket games) A shot that requires the cue ball to drive the object ball other than straight ahead. (See *cut shot*.)

APEX OF TRIANGLE. (Pocket games) The position in the grouping of object balls that is on the *foot spot*; the front ball position of the *pyramid* or *rack*.

AROUND THE TABLE. (Carom games) Describes shots in which the cue ball contacts three or more cushions, usually including the two short cushions, in an effort to score.

BALANCE POINT. (General) The point on a cue at which it would remain level if held by a single support, usually about 18" from the butt end of the cue.

BALL IN HAND. (Pocket games) See *cue ball in hand*.

BALL ON. (Snooker) A colored (non-red) ball a player intends to legally pocket; same as *on ball*.

BANK SHOT. (Pocket games) A shot in which the object ball is driven to one or more cushions before it is pocketed; incidental contact as a ball moves along and adjacent to a cushion does not qualify as a cushion or bank. It is not an obvious shot and must be called in games requiring called shots. (See *kick shot*.)

BAULK. (Snooker) The intervening space between the bottom cushion and the Baulk-line.

BAULK-LINE. (Snooker) A straight line drawn 29" from the face of the bottom cushion and parallel to it.

BED OF TABLE. (General) The flat, cloth-covered surface of the table within the cushions; the playing area exclusive of the cushions.

BILLIARD. (Carom games) A count or score; a successful shot.

BLIND DRAW. (General) A method used to determine pairings or bracketing of players in tournaments that assures totally random placement or pairing of contestants.

BOTTLE. (Pocket games) A specially shaped leather or plastic container used in various games. (Also called the *shake bottle*.)

BOTTOM CUSHION. (Snooker) The cushion located at the head of a snooker table — closest to the D.

BREAK. (Pocket games) See *open break* and *opening break shot*.

BREAK. (Snooker) Total scored in one inning.

BREAKING VIOLATION. (Pocket games) A violation of special rules which apply only to the *opening break* shot of certain games. Unless specified in individual game rules, a breaking violation is not a foul.

BRIDGE. (General) The hand configuration that holds and guides the shaft-end of the cue during play. (See *mechanical bridge*.)

BURST. (Forty-One Pocket Billiards) Scoring a total of more than 41 points.

BUTT OF CUE. (General) The larger end of a cue, opposite the tip. On a two-piece cue, the butt extends up to the joint.

CALL SHOT. (Pocket games) Requirement that a player designate, in advance of each shot, the ball to be made and the pocket into which it will be made. In calling the shot, it is NEVER necessary to indicate details such as the number of cushions, banks, kisses, caroms, etc.

CALLED BALL. (Pocket games) The ball the player has designated to be pocketed on a shot.

CALLED POCKET. (Pocket games) The pocket which a player has designated a ball to be shot.

CAROM. (General) To bounce off or glance off an object ball or cushion; a shot in which the cue ball bounces off one ball into another is termed a carom.

CAROM, SCORING. (General) Contact by the cue ball with object balls, the bottle or cushions in such a way that a legal score is made, according to specific game rules.

CENTER SPOT. (General) The exact center point of a table's playing surface.

CHALK. (General) A dry, slightly abrasive substance that is applied to the cue tip to help assure a non-slip contact between the cue tip and the cue ball.

CHUCK NURSE. (Straight Rail Billiards) A scoring technique used when one object ball rests against the cushion and the second object ball is to one side of the first ball and away from the cushion. Cue ball strikes the object ball at the cushion so that the cue ball just comes back to touch (carom) the second object ball without moving it out of position for a similar subsequent shot.

CLEAN BANK. (Bank Pocket Billiards) A shot in which the object ball being played does not touch any other object balls (i.e., no kisses, no combinations).

CLEAR BALL. (Carom games) The all-white ball, devoid of any markings, used in carom games. (See *spot ball*.)

COMBINATION. (Pocket games) Shot in which the cue ball first strikes a ball other than the one to be pocketed, with the ball initially contacted in turn striking one or more other balls in an effort to score.

COMBINATION ON. (Pocket games) Two or more balls positioned in such a way that a ball can be driven into a called pocket with a combination shot; often called a "dead combo" or an "on combo."

COMBINATION ON. (Snooker) See *plant*.

CONTACT POINT. (General) The precise point of contact between the cue ball and the object ball when the cue ball strikes the object ball. *(See **Instructional Playing Tips.**)*

CORNER-HOOKED. (Pocket games, Snooker) When the corner of a pocket prevents shooting the cue ball in a straight path directly to an object ball, the cue ball is corner-hooked; same as angled.

COUNT. (General) A score; a successful shot.

COUNT, THE. (General) The running score at any point during a player's inning in games where numerous points are scored successively.

CROSS CORNER. (Pocket games) Term used to describe a *bank shot* that will rebound from a cushion and into a corner pocket.

CROSS SIDE. (Pocket games) Term used to describe a *bank shot* that will rebound from a cushion and into a side pocket.

CROSS TABLE SHOT. (Carom games) Shot in which scoring is accomplished by driving the cue ball across the table between the long cushions.

CROTCH. (Carom games) The corner area of a carom table. The four crotches are defined as those spaces within crotch lines drawn between points on the side and end cushions 4 1/2" from the corners of the playing surface to the cushions.

CRUTCH. (General) Slang term for the *mechanical bridge*.

CUE. (General) Tapered device, usually wooden, used to strike the cue ball to execute carom or pocket billiard shots. (Also called "cue stick.")

CUE BALL. (General) The white, unnumbered ball that is always struck by the cue during play.

CUE BALL IN HAND. (Pocket games) Cue ball may be put into play anywhere on the playing surface.

CUE BALL IN HAND BEHIND THE HEAD STRING. (Pocket games) Cue ball may be put into play anywhere between the head string and the cushion on the head end of the table not in contact with an object ball. (See Diagram 1, Pg. 8.)

CUE BALL IN HAND WITHIN THE D. (Snooker) The cue ball is in hand within the D when it has entered a pocket or has been forced off the table. The base of the cue ball may be placed anywhere within or on the D. It remains in hand until the player strikes the cue ball with the tip of the cue or a foul is committed while the ball is on the table.

CUE TIP. (General) A piece of specially processed leather attached to the shaft end of the cue that contacts the cue ball when a shot is executed.

CUSHION. (General) The cloth-covered rubber which borders the inside of the rails on carom and pocket billiard tables; together the cushions form the outer perimeter of the basic playing surface.

CUT SHOT. (Pocket games) A shot in which the cue ball contacts the object ball to one side or the other of full center, thus driving it in a direction other than that of the initial cue ball path. (See **Instructional Playing Tips.**)

D. (Snooker) An area, semi-circular in shape, with the straight side formed by the head string and the semi-circle being prescribed by an arc drawn with the head spot as the center point. The radius of the semi-circle is determined by the size of the table being used. (See Diagram 13, Pg. 95.)

DEAD BALL. (Pocket games) A cue ball stroked in such a manner that virtually all of the speed and/or spin of the cue ball is transferred to the object ball, the cue ball retaining very little or none after contact.

DEAD BALL SHOT. (Pocket games) A shot in which a *dead ball* stroke is employed; often called a *kill shot*, because of the relative lack of cue ball motion after contact with the object ball.

DEAD COMBINATION. (Pocket games) See *combination on.*

DIAMONDS. (General) Inlays or markings on the table rails that are used as reference or target points. The diamonds are essential for the utilization of numerous mathematical systems employed by carom and pocket games players. (See **The Diamond System.**)

DRAW SHOT. (General) A shot in which the cue ball is struck below centers with a stroke below center effecting underspin, resulting in the cue ball reversing direction after contact with the object ball, because of the underspin applied to the cue ball.

DROP POCKETS. (Pocket games) Type of pockets with no automatic return of the balls to the foot end of the table; balls must be removed manually.

DOUBLE DRAW SHOT. (General) A shot in which such extreme and effective draw stroke is employed that when the cue ball reverses direction after contact with the object ball into a cushion and rebounds, the underspin (draw) overcomes the direction and speed of the rebound, causing the cue ball to stop and reverse direction again.

DOUBLE ELIMINATION. (General) A tournament format in which a player is not eliminated until he has sustained two match losses.

DOUBLE HIT. (General) A shot on which the cue ball is struck twice by the cue tip on the same stroke. (See **General Rules of Pocket Billiards, Carom Billiards.**)

DOUBLE ROUND ROBIN. (General) A tournament format in which each contestant in a field plays each of the other players twice.

ENGLISH. (General) Side spin applied to the cue ball by striking it off center; used to alter the natural roll of the cue ball and/or the object ball.

FEATHER SHOT. (General) A shot in which the cue ball barely touches or grazes the object ball; an extremely thin cut.

FERRULE. (General) A piece of protective material (usually white ivory or plastic) at the end of the cue shaft, onto which the cue tip is attached.

FOLLOW SHOT. (General) A shot in which the cue ball is struck above center effecting overspin, resulting in the cue ball continuing in the same general direction of the stroke with the object ball. Because of the overspin applied to the cue ball, the speed of the cue ball will be faster than that of natural roll.

FOLLOW-THROUGH. (General) The movement of the cue after contact with the cue ball through the area previously occupied by the cue ball. (See **Instructional Playing Tips.**)

FOOT OF TABLE. (General) The end of a carom or pocket billiard table at which the balls are racked or positioned at the start of a game.

FOOT SPOT. (General) The point on the foot end of the table where imaginary lines drawn between the center diamonds of the short rails and the second diamonds of the long rails intersect. (See Diagram 1, Pg. 8.)

FOOT STRING. (General) A line on the foot end of the table between the second diamonds of the long rails, passing through the foot spot. (See Diagram 1, Pg. 8.)

FORCE. (General) The power applied on the stroke to the cue ball, which may result in distortion and altering of natural angles and action of the ball.

FORCE DRAW. (General) A draw shot with extreme underspin applied to the cue ball; usually refers to shots in which the cue ball first travels in the direction of the stroke for a distance before the underspin takes effect and the cue ball stops and then draws back in a generally opposite direction.

FORCE FOLLOW. (General) A follow shot with extreme overspin applied to the cue ball, with the term generally used in reference to shots in which the cue ball is shot directly at and then "through" an object ball, with a pronounced hesitation or stop before the overspin propels the cue ball forward in the general direction of the stroke.

FOUL. (General) An infraction of the rules of play, as defined in either the general or the specific game rules. (Not all rule infractions are fouls.) Fouls result in a penalty, also dependent on specific game rules.

FOUL STROKE. (General) A stroke on which a foul takes place.

FRAME. (Snooker) The equivalent of one game in snooker.

FREE BALL. (Snooker) After a foul, if the cue ball is snookered, the referee shall state "Free Ball." If the non-offending player takes the next stroke he may nominate any ball as on, and for this stroke, such ball shall be regarded as, and acquire the value of, the ball on. (See **International Snooker** rules.)

FREE BREAK. (Pocket games) An opening break shot in which a wide spread of the object balls may be achieved without penalty or risk. Free breaks are detailed in individual games rules.

FROZEN. (General) A ball touching another ball or cushion.

FULL BALL. (General) Contact of the cue ball with an object ball at a contact point on a line bisecting the centers of the cue ball and object ball. (See **Instructional Playing Tips.**)

GAME. The course of play that starts when the referee has finished racking the balls, and ends at the conclusion of a legal shot which pockets the last required ball.

GAME BALL. (General) The ball which, if pocketed legally, would produce victory in a game.

GATHER SHOT. (Carom games) A shot on which appropriate technique and speed are employed to drive one or more balls away from the other(s) in such a manner that when the stroke is complete, the balls have come back together closely enough to present a comparatively easy scoring opportunity for the next shot.

GRIP. (General) The manner in which the butt of the cue is held in the hand. (See **Instructional Playing Tips.**)

GULLY TABLE. (Pocket games) A table with pockets and a return system that delivers the balls as they are pocketed to a collection bin on the foot end of the table.

HANDICAPPING. (General) Modifications in the scoring and/or rules of games to enable players of differing abilities to compete on more even terms.

HEAD OF TABLE. (General) The end of a carom or pocket billiard table from which the opening break is performed; the end normally marked with the manufacturer's nameplate.

HEAD SPOT. (General) The point on the head of the table where imaginary lines drawn between the center diamonds of the short rails and the second diamonds of the long rails intersect. (See Diagram 1, Pg. 8.)

HEAD STRING. (General) A line on the head end of the table between the second diamonds of the long rails, passing through the head spot. (See Diagram 1, Pg. 8.)

HICKEY. (Snooker Golf) Any foul.

HIGH RUN. (14.1 Continuous) During a specified segment of play, the greatest number of balls scored in one turn (inning) at the table.

HOLD. (General) *English* which stops the cue ball from continuing the course of natural roll it would take after having been driven in a certain direction.

INNING. (General) A turn at the table by a player.

IN HAND. (Pocket games) See *cue ball in hand*.

IN HAND BEHIND THE HEAD STRING. (Pocket games) See *cue ball in hand behind the head string*.

IN-OFF. (Snooker) A losing hazard; that is, when the cue ball enters a pocket. The snooker equivalent of a scratch.

IN THE RACK. (Pocket games) A ball that would interfere with the reracking of the object balls in games that extend past one rack.

JAW. (Pocket games) The slanted part of the cushion that is cut at an angle to form the opening from the bed of the table into the pocket.

JAWED BALL. (Pocket games) Generally refers to a ball that fails to drop because it bounces back and forth against the jaws of a pocket.

JOINT. (General) On two-piece cues, the screw-and-thread device, approximately midway in the cue, that permits it to be broken down into two separate sections.

JUMP SHOT. (General) A shot in which the cue ball an object ball is caused to rise off the bed of the table.

JUMPED BALL. (General) A ball that has left and remained off the playing surface as the result of a stroke; a ball that is stroked in a manner which causes it to jump over another ball.

KEY BALL. (14.1 Continuous) The 14th ball of each rack; called the key ball because it is so critical in obtaining position for the all important first (or break) shot of each reracking of the balls.

KICK SHOT. (General) a shot in which the cue ball banks off a cushion(s) prior to making contact with an object ball or scoring.

KILL SHOT. (Pocket games) See *dead ball shot*.

KISS. (General) Contact between balls. (See *kiss shot*.)

KISS SHOT. (Pocket games) A shot in which more than one contact with object balls is made by the cue ball; for example, the cue ball might kiss from one object ball into another to score the latter ball. Shots in which object balls carom off one or more other object balls to be pocketed. (Also called *carom* shots.)

KISS-OUT. (General) Accidental contact between balls that causes a shot to fail.

KITCHEN. (Pocket games) A slang term used to describe the area of the table between the head string and the cushion on the head end of the table. (Also called the area behind the head string.)

LAG. (Carom games) A shot in which the cue ball is shot three or more cushions before contacting the object balls.

LAG FOR BREAK. (General) Procedure used to determine starting player of game. Each player shoots a ball from behind the head string to the foot cushion, attempting to return the ball as closely as possible to the head cushion. (See **General Rules of Pocket Billiards, Carom Billiards**.)

LEAVE. (Pocket games) The position of the balls after a player's shot.

LONG. (General) Usually refers to a ball which, due to english and speed, travels a path with wider angles than those that are standard for such a ball if struck with *natural english* and moderate speed.

LONG STRING. (Pocket games) A line drawn from the center of the foot cushion to the foot spot (and beyond if necessary) on which balls are spotted.

LOSING HAZARD. (Snooker) Occurs when the cue ball is pocketed after contact with an object ball.

LOT. (General) Procedures used, not involving billiard skills, to determine starting player or order of play in casual or non-tournament play. Common methods used are flipping coins, drawing straws, drawing cards, or drawing peas or pills.

MASSE SHOT. (General) A shot in which extreme *english* is applied to the cue ball by elevating the cue butt at an angle with the bed of the table of anywhere between 30 and 90 degrees.

MATCH. The course of play that starts when the players are ready to lag and ends when the deciding game ends.

MECHANICAL BRIDGE. (General) A grooved device mounted on a handle providing support for the shaft of the cue during shots difficult to reach with normal bridge hand. Also called a *crutch* or *rake*.

MISCUE. (General) A stroke which results in the cue tip contact with cue ball being faulty. Usually the cue tip slides off the cue ball without full transmission of the desired stroke.

MISS. (General) Failure to execute a completed shot.

NATURAL. (Carom games) A shot with only natural angle and stroke required for successful execution; a simple or easily visualized, and accomplished, scoring opportunity.

NATURAL ENGLISH. (General) Moderate sidespin applied to the cue ball that favors the direction of the cue ball path, giving the cue ball a natural roll and a bit more speed than a center hit.

NATURAL ROLL. (General) Movement of the cue ball with no *english* applied.

NIP DRAW. (General) A short, sharp stroke, employed when a normal *draw* stroke would result in a foul due to drawing the cue ball back into the cue tip.

NURSES. (Carom games) Techniques whereby the balls are kept close to the cushions and each other, creating a succession of relatively easy scoring opportunities.

OBJECT BALLS. (General) The balls other than the cue ball on a shot.

OBJECT BALL, THE (Pocket games) The particular object ball being played on a shot.

ON BALL. (Snooker) See *ball on*.

OPEN BREAK. (Pocket games) The requirement in certain games that a player must drive a minimum of four object balls out of the *rack* to the cushions in order for the shot to be legal.

OPENING BREAK SHOT. (General) The first shot of a game.

PEAS. (Pocket games) Small plastic or wooden balls numbered 1 through 15 or 16, use defined in specific game rules. (Called *pills*.)

PILLS. (Pocket games) See *peas*.

PLANT. (Snooker) A position of two or more red balls that allows a ball to be driven into a pocket with a *combination* shot.

POSITION. (General) The placement of the cue ball on each shot relative to the next planned shot.

POT. (Snooker) The pocketing of an object ball.

POWDER. (General) Talc or other fine, powdery substance used to facilitate free, easy movement of the cue shaft through the *bridge*.

POWER DRAW SHOT. (General) Extreme *draw* applied to the cue ball. (See *force draw*.)

PUSH SHOT. (General) A shot in which the cue tip maintains contact with the cue ball beyond the split second allowed for a normal and legally stroked shot.

PYRAMID. (Pocket games) Positioning of the object balls in a triangular grouping (with the front apex ball on the foot spot), used to begin many pocket billiard games.

PYRAMID SPOT. (Snooker) The same as the pink spot. The spot is marked midway between the center spot and the face of the top cushion.

RACE. (General) Pre-determined number of games necessary to win a match or set of games.

RACK. The triangular equipment used for gathering the balls into the formation required by the game being played.

RAILS. (General) The top surface of the table, not covered by cloth, from which the cushions protrude toward the playing surface. The head and foot rails are the short rails on those ends of the table; the right and left rails are the long rails, dictated by standing at the head end of the table and facing the foot end.

RED BALL. (Carom games) The red-colored object ball. (Also the name of a particular 3-cushion billiard game.)

REST. (Snooker) The mechanical bridge.

REVERSE ENGLISH. (General) Sidespin applied to the cue ball, that favors the opposite direction of the natural cue ball path, which causes it to rebound from an object ball or a cushion at a slower speed than it would if struck at the same speed and direction without *english*.

ROUND ROBIN. (General) A tournament format in which each contestant plays each of the other players once.

RUNNING ENGLISH. (General) Sidespin applied to the cue ball which causes it to rebound from an object ball or a cushion at a narrower angle and at a faster speed than it would if struck at the same speed and direction without *english*.

RUN. (General) The total of consecutive scores, points or counts made by a player in one *inning*. The term is also used to indicate the total number of full short-rack games won without a missed shot in a match or tournament.

SAFETY. (General) Defensive positioning of the balls so as to minimize the opponent's chances to score. (The nature and rules concerning safety play are decidedly different in specific games; see individual game rules regarding safety play.) Player's inning ends after a safety play.

SCRATCH. (Carom games) To score a point largely by accident, due to an unanticipated kiss, unplanned time-shot, etc.

SCRATCH. (Pocket games) The cue ball is going into a pocket on a stroke.

SEEDING. (General) Pre-determined initial pairings or advanced positioning of players in a field of tournament competition.

SET. (General) Pre-determined number of games necessary to win a match.

SHAFT. (General) The thinner part of a cue, on which the cue tip is attached. On a two-piece cue, the shaft extends from the *cue tip* to the *joint*.

SHAKE BOTTLE. (Pocket games) See *bottle*.

SHOT. An action that begins at the instant the cue tip contacts the cue ball, and ends when all balls in play stop rolling and spinning.

SHORT. (General) Usually refers to a ball which, due to *english* and *stroke*, travels a path with narrower angles than those for a ball struck without *english*.

SHORT-RACK. (Pocket games) Games which utilize fewer than 15 countable object balls.

SINGLE ELIMINATION. (General) A tournament format in which a single loss eliminates a player from the competition.

SNAKE. (Carom games) A shot in which the use of *english* causes the cue ball to make three or more cushion contacts, though utilizing only two different cushions.

SNOOKERED. (Snooker) The condition of incoming player's cue ball position when he cannot shoot in a straight line and contact all portions of an *on ball* directly facing the cue ball (because of balls not "on" that block the path). (Included for information only, since the rules of American Snooker in this book are of such nature that being snookered has no special impact on the game rules or play).

SPLIT DOUBLE ELIMINATION. (General) A modification of the *double elimination* tournament format, in which the field is divided into sections, with one player emerging from each of the sections to compete for the championship, in a single showdown match for the championship.

SPLIT HIT. A shot in which it cannot be determined which object ball(s) the cue ball contacted first, due to the close proximity of the object balls.

SPOT. (General) The thin, circular piece of cloth or paper glued onto the cloth to indicate the spot locality (i.e., head spot, center spot, foot spot); also an expression to describe a handicap.

SPOT BALL. (Carom games) The white ball differentiated from the clear by one or more markings; usually spots, dots or circles.

SPOT SHOT. (Pocket games) Player shoots a ball on the foot spot with the *cue ball in hand behind the head string.*

SPOTTING BALLS. (General) Replacing balls to the table in positions as dictated by specific game rules.

STANCE. (General) The position of the body during shooting. (See **Instructional Playing Tips.**)

STOP SHOT. (Pocket games) A shot in which the cue ball stops immediately upon striking the object ball.

STRIKER. (Snooker) The player who is about to shoot and has yet to complete his *inning.*

STROKE. (General) The movement of the cue as a shot is executed. (See **Instructional Playing Tips.**)

SUCCESSIVE FOULS. (Pocket games) Fouls made on consecutive strokes by the same player, also called *consecutive fouls.*

TABLE IN POSITION. (General) Term used to indicate that the object balls remain unmoved following a shot.

THROW SHOT. (Pocket games) 1. A *cut shot* that alters the path of the ball by applying *english.* 2. A combination shot of frozen or near frozen object balls that is struck by the cue ball left or right of center on the first object ball, thus causing the second (or played) object ball to travel in the opposite direction of the cue ball hit.

TIME SHOT. (General) A shot in which the cue ball (most often) moves another ball into a different position and then continues on to meet one of the moved balls for a score.

TOP CUSHION. (Snooker) The cushion located at the foot of a snooker table — closest to the black spot.

TRIANGLE. (Pocket games) The triangular device used to place the balls in position for the start of most games.

YELLOW BALL. (Carom games) In international competition the spot ball has been replaced by a yellow ball without any markings.

INSTRUCTIONAL PLAYING TIPS

By Jerry Briesath, Richard Rhorer

There are many variations of the game of billiards, but the fundamentals of good billiard playing are inherent in every format of the sport. This section deals with these fundamentals.

CUE SELECTION: Try several cues and start with the one that feels most comfortable to you. It is difficult for a beginning pool player to know which weight cue to get. Keep in mind that most professional pool players use a cue that weighs between 18 and 20 ounces. The shaft size of a cue mainly has to do with personal preference and the size of your fingers. Shaft sizes for pool cues basically run between 12 to 14 millimeters. Most professional pool players play with a shaft size of $12^{1}/_{2}$ to $13^{1}/_{2}$ mm.

PROPER GRIP OF A CUE:
Hold the cue lightly with the thumb and first three finger (Figure 1). When the cue is gripped properly, it should not touch the palm of your hand (Figure 2). It is very important to maintain a light grip on the cue at all times. Gripping the cue too tightly while stroking through the cue ball is a common mistake that must be corrected.

Figure 1   **Figure 2**

WHERE TO GRIP THE
CUE: When you are bent over in your shooting position and the cue tip is almost touching the cue ball, the shooting hand should be directly under the elbow. It is okay to have the shooting hand an inch or two ahead of the elbow at impact. It is never recommended to have the shooting hand behind the elbow at impact (Figure 3).

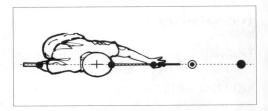

Figure 3

The following Instructions and Illustrations are for Right Handed Players

CUE STANCE: Face the shot. Before you even bend over to shoot, there is a line up of three points—the chin, the cue ball and the exact place you want the cue ball to go. Turn your body slightly to the right without your chin is leaving the point of line up. Bend over at the waist, put your bridge hand down 7 to 10 inches from the cue ball so that your chin is 2 to 8 inches directly above the cue stick. Adjust your feet to distribute your body weight approximately 50/50 (as shown in Figure 4). A generally accepted stance when you are in your shooting position is to have the tip of the right toe directly under the line of the cue and the left toe slightly to the left side of the line of the cue. This should allow a 4 to 6 inch gap between the hip and the cue for freedom of movement.

Figure 4

A common mistake made by beginners in their shooting position is to have the shoulders and chest facing the cue ball. A preferred technique is to turn the left shoulder out in front and the right shoulder back thus turning the chest more to the right. This makes a better body alignment (Figure 5).

Figure 5

BRIDGES: One of the most overlooked fundamentals of the game is a solid bridge. The difference between a good billiard player and just another billiard

Figure 6

Figure 7

player can often be traced to the bridge or their bridges. Nothing is of greater importance in billiard play. If the shot you are executing is to be accurate, your bridge must be natural, yet give firm guidance to the cue. Adapt the following formulas for your correct bridges. There are two basic bridges–an open bridge and a closed bridge.

Open Bridge: An open bridge is one formed by placing the hand firmly on the table, cupping the hand, pressing the thumb against the forefinger forming a "V" (Figure 6). The cue is now placed on the "V" (Figure 7). To adjust the height of the bridge, simply pull the fingers toward you to raise the bridge (Figure 8), or pushing the fingers away to lower the bridge (Figure 9). This allows you to strike the cue ball high, medium or low while maintaining a solid bridge. This bridge is highly recommended for beginners. Profession-

Figure 8   **Figure 9**

als use this bridge on many shots that don't require a lot of power or cue ball spin.

Stretch Shots: When stretching out for a shot where a long bridge is required (12 inches or more), it is very important to use an open bridge. Keep the backswing and follow-through very short and use minimum speed (Figure 10).

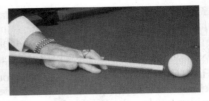

Closed Bridge: Place your entire bridge hand flat on the table. The heel of your hand should be down firmly (Figure 11). Bend your forefinger so that its tip touches your thumb, thus forming a loop (Figure 12). Place the cue tip in the loop formed by forefinger and thumb, resting the cue against the inner groove of these two

Figure 10

fingers. Extend the cue through the loop formed by the above. Now pull your

Figure 11

forefinger firmly against the cue, but with the loop just loose enough so that you can stroke the cue back and forth easily. As you do the above, keep your middle, ring and small fingers spread out and firmly pressed against the table. They form the bridge tripod which must be firm yet natural. You have the correct bridge when the cue passes through easily, accurately and with firm guidance and support.

Figure 12

The bridge length is the distance between the loop of the forefinger and the cue ball on a closed bridge or the thumb and the cue ball on an open bridge. Most professional pool players use a bridge length of 7 to 10 inches. Whether you use an open or a closed bridge, the heel of your hand should be firmly on the table at all times. The bridge hand must not move while you are striking the ball.

Bridge for Follow Shot: Using a Standard Bridge, elevate the tripod fingers slightly. Keep the cue level (Figure 13).

Figure 13

Bridge for Draw Shot: Using a Standard Bridge, lower the tripod fingers until your thumb rests on the bed of the table. Keep the cue level (Figure 14).

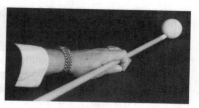

Figure 14

Rail Bridges: If the cue ball is four inches or more away from the rail, set your bridge hand on the rail. Place your thumb under the index finger (Figure 15). Put the cue on the rail against the thumb, and bring your forefinger over the shaft (Figure 16). Keep your cue as level as possible when stroking your shot.

If the cue ball is closer than 4 inches to the rail, place the cue between the thumb and forefinger. Place the other three fingers on the rail (Figure 17).

Figure 15   **Figure 16**

Bridge for Over Ball Shot: When it is necessary to shoot over an object ball in order to stroke the cue ball, the following bridge should be employed. Bracing all four of your fingers on the bed of the table behind the obstructing object ball(s), raise the hand as high as necessary and place the cue on the support made by your index finger joint and the thumb (Figures 18 and 19). This is an uncomfortable bridge, but a very necessary one and should be practiced.

Figure 17

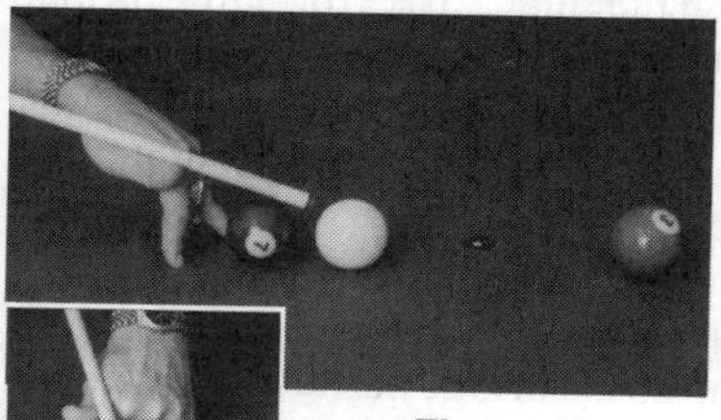

Mechanical Bridges: If a shot is beyond reach with any of the above mentioned bridges, a mechanical bridge should be employed. Don't sacrifice a shot because you cannot use the mechanical bridge; it is very easy. Set the bridge on the table 6 to 8 inches from the cue ball. Place your hand on the bridge. Place the shaft of your cue in the notch at the front part of the bridge. (Use higher notch for "follow," lower notch for "draw" or "stop.") Place your thumb under the base of the cue and your four fingers over the top of the cue. Your elbow will be sticking out to the side as you stroke; the bridge will be to the left if you are right-handed. Be sure to lay the bridge flat on the table if possible (Figure 20) and secure it with your left hand. Now use the same system as for any other shot.

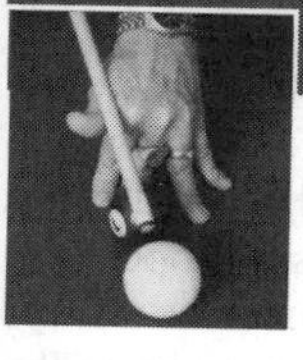

Figure 18

Figure 19

Figure 20

LEARNING A STROKE

Remember, "Practice doesn't make Perfect; *Perfect Practice* makes Perfect." A stroke is a throwing motion. A good throwing motion starts with a slow backswing with a smooth acceleration through the cue ball. A common mistake by amateur and beginning players is to drop the elbow while stroking through the cue ball. It's important to note that the *throwing* motion must take place only in that part of the arm below the elbow. The less the elbow moves up and down, the more precise the stroke. It should be a pendulum swing from the elbow down.

CUEING THE BALL

For the beginning player, it is important to adjust the bridge so that the cue tip strikes the cue ball a little above center, never to the left or right, while he is learning accuracy and speed control. As his skill level progresses, it will be necessary for him to learn to strike the cue ball at other places–higher, lower, left, right, etc.

The most important three things to learn after a player has progressed past the beginner stage are (1) how to make the cue ball follow, (2) how to stop the cue ball on a straight-in shot and (3) how to make the cue ball draw or reverse direction off the object ball. (See Figure 21 for further details.) The smoother the stroke, the lower or higher the cue ball may be struck without miscueing. Most good players can strike the cue ball almost two full tips off center without miscueing.

Keep in mind that extreme spin requires a very good stroke and smooth delivery. When following the cue ball the higher the tip strikes the cue ball the more overspin imparted to the cue ball; likewise for backspin. In pool there is one stroke. You use the same stroke to follow the ball as you do to stop or draw the cue ball.

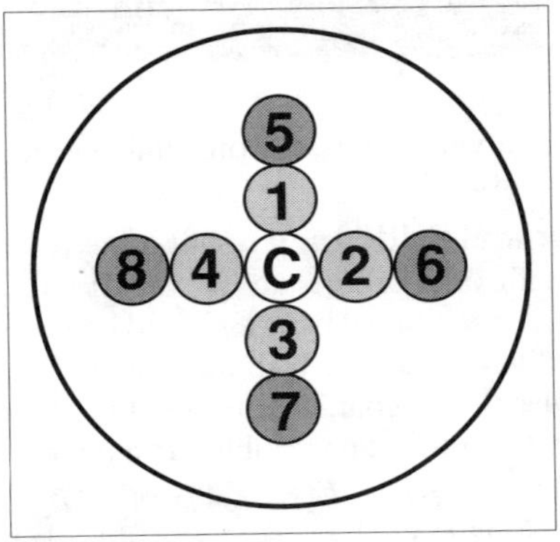

A common mistake for people is that when they want to stop or draw the cue ball, they think they have to *jab* or hit the cue ball and stop the cue tip immediately on impact with the cue ball or even hit the cue ball and pull the stick back. That is not the way to stop or draw the cue ball. To make the cue ball stop, you must put enough back spin on it by shooting below center to cause it to arrive at the object ball with no spin. The cloth is always trying to rub the backspin off the cue ball. The farther the cue ball is from the object ball, the lower or harder you must shoot to cause the cue ball to stop or come back. (Figure 21 shows positions 1-4 and also 5-8, extreme spin.) When using backspin on the cue ball, it is important to understand the concept that the backspin you put on the cue ball is caused by the tremendous friction the chalk creates between the tip and the cue ball. You must understand that the cue stick imparts backspin to the cue ball as you *throw* it 4 to 6 inches through

Figure 21

the lower part of the cue ball. (Figure 22 shows how the cue stick follows through 4 to 6 inches after contact with the object ball.)

HITTING THE OBJECT BALL

The first thing the pocket billiard player must learn is that his eyes should be on the object ball as he executes the shot. During the aiming process his eyes go back and forth between the cue ball and the object ball. When you are ready to pocket the object ball, your eyes are on the object ball.

Figure 22

To shoot a ball into a pocket, the simplest way to determine your point of impact on the object ball is to draw an imaginary line from the center of the pocket and bisects the object ball. Where this line extends through the object ball is your contact point. It is the point at which the edge of the cue ball must contact the edge of the object ball. You must aim so that these two contact points will meet (Figure 23).

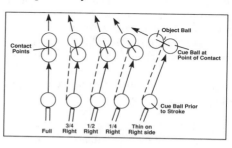

Figure 23

Figure 24

Figure 25

POINT OF AIM, POINT OF IMPACT

In Figures 24 and 25 you can see there is a white dot on the object ball. This mark is where the cue ball must contact the object ball in order to pocket the ball. The white dot is called the Point of Impact. The white dot on the table is the Point of Aim. No matter where the cue ball is the cue stick and the center of the cue ball are aimed at the Point of Aim in order to contact the Point of Impact on the object ball.

A keen eye and judgement are important here. Your skill in hitting the Point of Aim will determine your status in pocket billiard circles.

Once again there is no better experience than practice. Accomplish this phase by placing your cue ball close to the object ball, then gradually increase the distance between the two balls. Time and practice will increase your accuracy in striking the cue ball correctly and hitting the object ball where you aim, thus driving it to the exact target area desired.

LEARNING A GOOD SHOOTING SYSTEM

The first thing you have to remember when you play pool is that you don't control the balls. All you control is your body and your cue. What the balls do is only a result of how well your body moves the cue. There are two things you have to get out of the way before you can shoot any shot. You have to make sure the cue is aiming straight and you have to make sure your arm can move the cue straight back and forth the full length of your bridge (7 to 10 inches).

A good practice technique for this is to place the cue ball on the spot and shoot it down the table into a corner pocket. Be sure to get your stance and aim correct. Then take a couple of smooth, slow warm-up swings the full length of the bridge. Stop at the cue ball and check your aim by letting your eyes go down the line of the cue to the target and back a couple of times. If the aim looks perfect, lock your eyes on the target, then after a slow backswing, "throw" the cue smoothly 4 to 6 inches through the cue ball directly over the dot. If after executing the shot, the cue is to the left or right of the dot, repeat this system until you can shoot the ball into the pocket and the cue finishes its motion 4 to 6 inches straight ahead and directly over the dot. It is *imperative* that your head remain perfectly still during the shot. This is an important practice to help in developing your accuracy and stroke.

The warm-up swings should be slow and smooth in both directions, training the arm to make the cue go straight. After every two or three warm-up strokes, be sure to stop at the cue ball and check your aim. If it looks perfect, take a smooth backswing, and then accelerate 4 to 6 inches through the cue ball at any speed you want to shoot. It is very important that you always maintain the same slow backswing no matter how hard you accelerate through the ball. Never go back faster just because you want to shoot harder. Its just like throwing a ball; to be accurate, you go back slowly, then you throw hard.

It is important to learn to stroke through the ball at all speeds. Although you have more control at slower speeds, sometimes position play will require you to shoot a ball harder. Keep in mind–slow backswing, accelerate forward.

ENGLISH (Left or Right)

When we talk about *english*, we are generally referring to left or right spin on the cue ball. By putting left or right spin on the cue ball, you immediately do three things that can cause you to miss a shot. Beginning with right hand english, when you strike the cue ball on the right hand side, the cue ball (1) immediately deflects off the tip to the left of the line of the cue stick. As the cue ball proceeds down the table, it may (2) curve back to the right just a little bit. It will never curve back as much as it deflects unless you elevate the cue, which we're not going to talk about here. With a level cue and right hand english on the ball, it will first deflect to the left. It might curve back a little to the right depending on the distance. The third thing is that the english might *throw* the object ball. Right hand english can throw the object ball a little to the left of the contact line. The curve back is dependent on the speed and the distance that the cue ball is traveling.

We mention three things that happen when you use right hand english, the deflection immediately off the tip, the curve back to the right and the throwing the object ball to the left. Of these three, the curve is usually very slight. The throwing of the object ball is very slight. The biggest factor in causing people to miss with english is the *deflection* off the cue tip. It is important to remember when using right hand english, aim slightly to the right of where you would normally aim on the object ball. When using left hand english, you must aim slightly to the left of where you would normally aim on the object ball.

Left or right hand english is almost never used to pocket an object ball, but rather for playing position on another object ball. The purpose of applying sidespin to the cue ball is to change the angle at which the cue ball comes off a rail after striking the object ball. Always remember, never use english to make balls, *only* to play position on the next ball. Although english is extremely important in playing position, the pros will tell you, "the less english you use the less often you get in trouble" (Chart A).

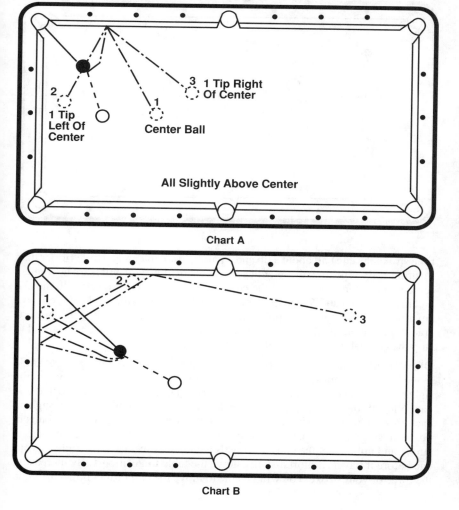

3 1 Tip Right Of Center

2

1 Tip Left Of Center

1

Center Ball

All Slightly Above Center

Chart A

Chart B

Follow Shots: Set up the balls as in Chart B. By stroking the cue ball between a tip and a tip and a half above center, the cue ball will follow to Position 1. Then set up the same shot and stroke the cue ball at the same height, add some power and see that the cue ball will end up in Position 2. Now stroke the cue ball again in the same position, but with an even firmer stroke to see the cue ball respond as in Postition 3 on the Chart.

Stop Shots: Place the balls on the table as in Chart C. Strike the cue ball about a tip below center. Use a smooth stroke and practice stopping the cue ball as it contacts the object ball. Do this a few times to get the feel of how hard you shoot, then practice shooting this same shot a little lower on the cue ball with a little less speed and see if you can still get the same results. Then proceed to Postition 2. This

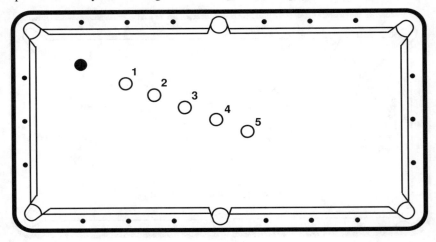

Chart C

time stroke the cue ball about a tip and a half below center and a little firmer than Position 1. By repeating this practice in a new position, you will learn how much force you need in order to stop the cue ball. Continue this practice with the cue ball in Positions 3 and 4 each time increasing the power of the stroke. If you have any difficulty at a particular position, repeat that practice until it feels comfortable. Remember, the lower you strike the cue ball, the less power is required to stop the cue ball on contact with the object ball.

Draw Shots: Place the balls as shown in Chart D. Notice there is a *slight* angle in the ball placement so that when you draw the cue ball it will move over to the right slightly and then come back past your cue. The reason for this is so that you can follow through the cue ball 4 to 6 inches to practice a good follow-through on each shot without worrying about the cue ball hitting your cue. With the balls in position, strike the cue ball about a tip and a half below center with a moderate stroke and notice that the cue ball travels a couple of inches to the right of your cue before it travels a short distance down the table to Position 1. By increasing the force of your stroke, you will be able to move the ball farther down the table

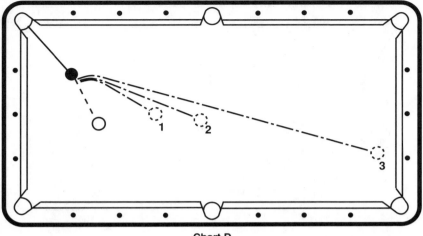

Chart D

toward Positions 2 and 3. It is important on all these exercises to be sure the cue tip follows through 4 to 6 inches. If you shoot the cue ball for any stop or draw shot, the cue ball is struck one to one and a half tips below center. When the pendelum motion of the arm is correct, the cue tip will follow through 4 to 6 inches past the object ball, and continue in a slightly downward motion, ending up touching the cloth.

Position Play: Players are forever trying to play position—that is, making an easy shot and making the cue ball arrrive at a place on the table to have another easy shot. The two secrets of playing proper position are (1) memory and (2) speed control. When a beginner is learning to play, he should repeat the same shots over and over. Not only do you watch the object ball being pocketed, but the path of the cue ball after contacting the object ball. If you are continually hitting the cue ball a little above center, the cue ball will always take virtually the same path. Fifty percent of position play is remembering where the cue ball went after that particular shot. The other fifty percent of position play is the speed control of the cue ball.

The most important and easiest way a beginner can learn position is to set up a shot (as in Chart E). When you set up a practice shot, mark the cloth with a chalk dot under the object ball and also the cue ball so you start at the same position each time. Pocket the object ball by hitting a little above center and watch where the cue ball hits the first rail and the direction it takes coming off that rail. By shooting this shot several times at different speeds, but striking the cue ball in the same spot each time, you will notice the path of the cue ball will follow in almost the same line each time you shoot. To improve your game, work on playing position on each of the shots in the diagram by varying the speed at which you strike the cue ball.

Now if you set the balls up in the same position and strike the cue ball a little below center, you will notice that the path of the cue ball will be completely different off the object ball. Repeat this several times, until you can make the cue

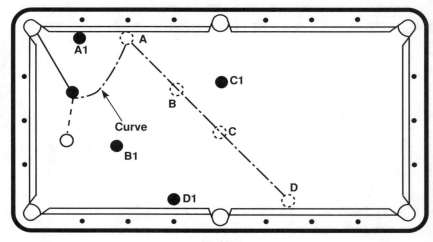

Chart E

ball go in the same direction, but travel farther down the table depending on the speed of your stroke. After setting up these shots and executing them by hitting the ball a little below center, set them up again and strike the cue ball even farther below center. This is a good exercise to learn the basics of what happens when you shoot the cue ball at different heights and speeds.

EXERCISES

FOLLOW, STOP AND DRAW: This exercise is to show you the different ways the cue ball will react when it is cued at different levels. Set up the shot in Chart F. The object ball is about a diamond out and directly in line between the two side pockets. The cue ball is at a slight angle toward the diamond past the

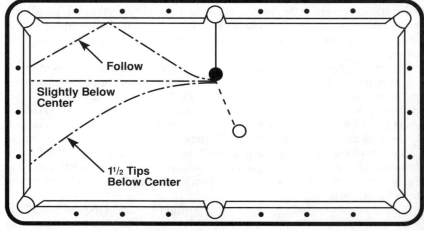

Chart F

side pocket. When you hit the cue ball with follow, the cue ball will take a slight curve as shown in the path in the diagram. If you hit the cue ball slightly below center, it will go almost straight down the table. If the cue ball is hit about one and a half tips below center, it will curve back more toward the corner pocket.

POSITION EXERCISE: Learning Position Play is learning the easiest way to get the balls off the table. The best way to learn that is an exercise we call 3-Ball, Ball in Hand. This is one of the best exercises to improve your skill level in control and position. Throw three balls on the table. In chart G, we see balls 1, 2 and 3. This numeric order is the easiest way to play off these balls by placing the cue ball as shown. Striking the cue ball above center on the 1-ball, you can see by the path of the cue ball that it will follow into the rail and then head right toward the 2-ball. By going to the rail after pocketing the 1-ball and depending on your speed of stroke, you can end up in any of the three cue ball positions. It is very difficult to make a mistake. This is what pros look for: the easiest way to get position on their next ball. If you shoot the cue ball again above center and pocket the 2-ball,

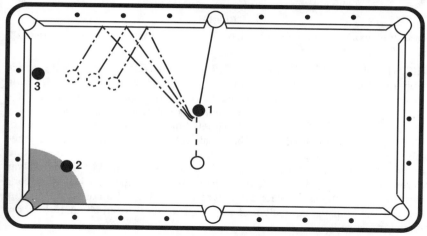

Chart G

the cue ball ends up anywhere within the darkened circle around the 2-ball. Then the 3-ball is an easily pocketed shot.

One of the best ways of improving your game of pool is by repeating shots. Don't repeat long, difficult shots. The ones to repeat are the easy and semi-easy ones that are frequently missed. For the more proficient players, even if you make the object ball and fail to get position, repeat that same shot until you feel comfortable that you can make that ball and get position.

Most people think that if they could make tough shots, they would be better players. The reality is that games are not won by people who make the tough shots; games are lost by players who miss shots that are very easy.

Chart H shows the many ways the speed of stroke can be used to play position. By using a soft stroke, you can play shape to position A to play A1 for your next shot. A slightly harder stroke will go to position B for B1 as the next shot.

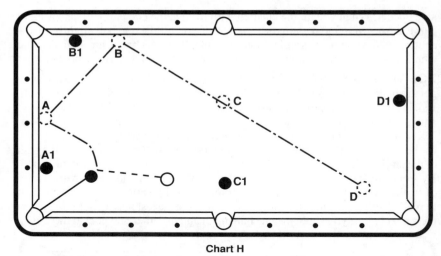

Chart H

Continue working on your speed of stroke until you can play position on shots C1 and D1.

EIGHT BALL AND NINE BALL, BALL IN HAND: Another great practice technique for beginners or stronger players is to play Eight Ball or Nine Ball with a rule change. When a person breaks and a ball is made on the break, he can take "Ball in Hand" anywhere on the table and shoot until he misses. The incoming player also takes "ball in hand" and shoots until he misses. The advantage of playing this way is that when you have ball in hand every time you come to the table, you start looking over the table. Even a beginner will start to see patterns of two or maybe three balls. The better player learns very quickly the easiest way to run the balls off. It trains you to see patterns and see the easy way to go for a run out. By playing Ball in Hand pool whether it is Eight Ball or Nine Ball, you learn in one hour the equivalent of what you would learn in about 15 hours of regular practice.

BALL IN HAND EQUAL OFFENSE: Another great practice game is a variation of Equal Offense which is also in this book. In Equal Offense each ball is one point and you can shoot at any ball. No balls count on the break. After the break, the same player who breaks gets ball in hand three times per rack. After each miss, he gets ball in hand again. Then he records how many balls he made that rack. A perfect score is 150 points in 10 racks. By playing this 3-Miss way, a person learns to see and play simple patterns. When a person's score approaches 130 or more in ten racks, then he progresses to the 2-Miss level. Now he breaks the balls and after the break, he gets ball in hand twice per rack. When his score improves again to 130 or more in ten racks, then he is playing well enough to progress to the 1-Miss level. Any player who shoots 130 points or more on the 1-Miss level is a very good amateur player. This is a great practice game.

THROW SHOTS: (Charts I, J, K, L) The object of a "throw" shot is to provide force or english that will move an object ball along an off-center path when two balls are *frozen*.

This situation often arises when the cue ball is touching (frozen) to an object ball. If the two are in alignment with a pocket, there is no problem. If not in alignment, it is still possible to pocket the object ball by using a "throw shot" which spins the object ball to the left or right. Chart I shows how, by hitting the cue ball on the left side, the object ball is thrown to the right side. Chart J illustrates that striking the cue ball on the right side moves the object ball to the left.

Another version of the throw shot is when two object balls are frozen together. The cue ball is free, but not in position to pocket either ball easily. In this case, the cue ball (hit without english) strikes the closest object ball on either the right

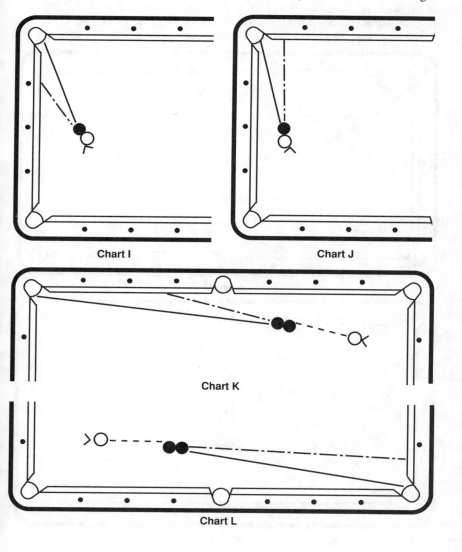

Chart I

Chart J

Chart K

Chart L

side (Chart K) or the left side (Chart L) to throw the second object ball in the opposite direction.

Kiss Shots: (Chart M & N) The object of this exercise is to pocket one of two balls that are frozen together without the use of english. When two balls are frozen together, an axis or center line is established by their relationship. A cue extended along this imaginary line will readily determine if the closest object ball, when struck on the back half, will follow the line into a pocket. If the cue does not point to a pocket, the object ball will not go into a pocket.

Chart M shows how this kiss shot can be made from either side. Chart N demonstrates that one object ball can be pocketed. The other cannot. Arrange two balls in various frozen positions and practice finding the center line. Then, mix throw shots with kiss shots to increase your options under these conditions.

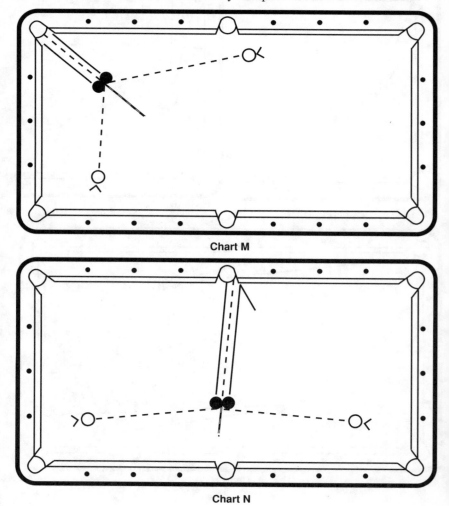

Chart M

Chart N

Rules for Tournament Play

The following rules concern the play, scoring, officiating and responsibilities for tournament competition in all pocket billiard games. However, the precepts and principles of these rules are to be considered part of the games' General Rules and should be applied as appropriate to all play, whether or not a formal tournament.

For purposes of simplicity and clarity, masculine pronouns have been utilized throughout these rules. Such references apply to any player or teams of players.

1.1. PLAYER RESPONSIBILITY. It is the player's responsibility to be aware of all rules, regulations and schedules applying to his competition. While tournament officials will make every reasonable effort to have such information readily available to all players as appropriate, the ultimate responsibility rests with the player himself. (For exceptions to this rule see: Rule 2.16..) The player has no recourse if such information is not volunteered; the responsibility for knowing his situation and/or the rules lies with the player himself.

1.2. ACCEPTANCE OF EQUIPMENT. Tournament players should assure themselves, prior to beginning play, that the balls and other equipment are standard and legal. Once they begin play of a match, they may no longer question the legality of the equipment in use (unless the opponent **and** tournament officials both agree with the objection **and** any available remedy proposed by the tournament officials).

1.3. USE OF EQUIPMENT. Players may not use equipment or accessory items for purposes or in a manner other than those for which the items were intended. For example, powder containers, chalk cubes, etc., may not be used to prop up a *mechanical bridge* (or natural hand bridge); no more than two mechanical bridges may be used at one time, nor may they be used to support anything other than the *cue shaft*. Extra or out-of-play balls may not be used by players to check clearances or for any other reason (except to lag for break); the triangle may be employed by players to ascertain whether a ball is in the rack when a match is unofficiated and the table has not been pencil-marked around the triangle area.

1.4. EQUIPMENT RESTRICTIONS. Players may use chalk, powder, mechanical bridge(s) and cue of their choice or design. However, tournament officials may restrict a player if he attempts action that is disruptive of either the house equipment or normal competitive conditions. As examples, a player may be restrained from using red chalk on green cloth; he may be advised not to use powder in such an excessive fashion as to unduly affect the balls or table cloth; he may be barred from using a cue with a noise-making device that is clearly disruptive to other competitors.

1.5. MARKING OF TABLES. When racking the balls a triangle must be used. Prior to competition, each table and the triangle to be used on it shall be marked so as to ensure that the same triangle will be used throughout the tournament on the same table.

An accurate and clearly visible pencil line must also be marked on the cloth: (1) around the outer edge of the triangle to ensure accurate and consistent placement to enable accurate judgement as to ball positions; (2) on the long string to enable accurate spotting of balls; and (3) on the head string to facilitate determinations of whether balls are behind the head string.

The *head spot, center spot* and *foot spot* must also be determined to be accurately marked, whether with discreet penciled "plus" marks, or with standard spots if being employed.

1.6. ADMINISTRATIVE DISCRETION. The management of each tournament shall reserve the right to set forth rules and procedures appropriate and reasonable for the particular tournament involved, such as may regard players' dress requirements, method of receiving entry fees, refund policy of entry fees, scheduling flexibility, pairing procedures, etc.

However, for tournaments to receive a BCA, WPA, WPBA or PBTA sanction, certain requirements must be met, primarily with regard to safeguarding and ensuring proper distribution of the prize fund.

1.7. LATE START. A player must be ready to begin a match within fifteen minutes of the start of the match, or his opponent wins by forfeit. The starting time is considered to be the scheduled time or the time the match is announced, whichever is later.

1.8. NO PRACTICE DURING MATCH. While a match is in progress, practice is not allowed. Taking a shot that is not part of that game is a foul.

1.9. ASSISTANCE NOT ALLOWED. While a match is in progress, players are not allowed to ask spectators for assistance in planning or executing shots. If a player asks for and receives such assistance, he loses the game. Any spectator who spontaneously offers any significant help to a player will be removed from the area.

1.10. FAILURE TO LEAVE THE TABLE. When a player's inning comes to an end, the player must discontinue shooting. Failure to do so is loss of game (exception in 14.1 - ruled as "deliberate foul").

1.11. SLOW PLAY. If in the opinion of the referee a player is impeding the progress of the tournament or game with consistently slow play, the referee can warn the player and then at his discretion impose a maximum one minute time limit for that person between shots. If the referee does impose a one minute time limit and that limit is exceeded, a foul will be called and the incoming player is rewarded according to the rules applicable to the game being played.

If a shot-clock is used, and the player exceeds the time limit specified for the tournament, a foul will be called and the incoming player is rewarded according to the rules applicable to the game being played.

1.12. SUSPENDED PLAY. If a player shoots while play is suspended by the referee, he loses the game. Announcement of the suspension is considered sufficient warning.

1.13. TIME OUT. A player is only allowed to take a time out during his/her turn at the table or between sets (if a format with sets is used). During a time out, a sign should be placed on the table by the referee, and no practice will be allowed on that table. In general, each player will be allowed one time out per match, and a maximum of 5 minutes per time out. When a format with sets is used, each player will be allowed one time out in the final set (in the third set if playing best-of-3, or in the fifth set if playing the best-of-5 sets). This final-set rule applies regardless of whether a player has taken a time out in an earlier set.

1.14. CONCESSION. If a player concedes, he loses the game. The unscrewing of a jointed cue stick, except to replace a shaft, is considered to be a concession. No warning from the referee is required in the case of a concession.

1.15. SCORING OF FORFEITS. Matches forfeited for any reason under these rules shall not result in any scores being included in the statistics of a tournament, regardless of whether any score had been reached prior to the declaration of forfeiture. For official records, no point scores should be recorded, but rather the notations "W(F)" and "L(F)" as appropriate should be employed. (Matches lost through disqualification are considered forfeits for purposes of this rule.)

If, however, the player awarded a match through his opponent's forfeiture has posted a high run (or similar accomplishment for which an award is granted) during play of the match prior to declaration of forfeiture, that high run or other mark shall be eligible for the tournament award or prize.

1.16. PLAYING WITHOUT A REFEREE. When a referee is not available, the player who is not shooting will assume the duties of the referee to the extent of play on the table.

1.16.1. CUE BALL FOULS ONLY. When a referee is presiding over a match, it is a foul for a player to touch any ball (cue ball or object ball) with the cue, clothing, body, mechanical bridge or chalk, before, during or after a shot. However, when a referee is not presiding over a game, it is not a foul to accidentally touch stationary object balls while in the act of shooting. If such an accident occurs, the player should allow the Tournament Director to restore the object balls to their correct positions. If the player does not allow such a restoration, and a ball set in motion as a normal part of the shot touches such an unrestored ball, or passes partly into a region originally occupied by a disturbed ball, the shot is a foul. In short, if the accident has any effect on the outcome of the shot, it is a foul. In any case, the Tournament Director must be called upon to restore the positions of the disturbed balls as soon as possible, but not during the shot. It is a foul to play another shot before the Tournament Director has restored any accidentally moved balls.

At the nonshooting player's option, the disturbed balls will be left in their new positions. In this case, the balls are considered restored, and subsequent contact on them is not a foul.

It is still a foul to make any contact with the cue ball whatsoever while it is in play.

1.16.2. THIRD OPINION. When a shot comes up that seems likely to lead to controversy, the player not shooting should temporarily enlist a tournament official or a third party to judge the legality of the execution.

1.16.3. RESOLVING DISPUTES. Any dispute between the two players will be resolved by the tournament director or his appointed substitute.

1.16.4. SPLIT HITS. If the cue ball strikes a legal object ball and a non-legal object ball at approximately the same instant , and it cannot be determined which ball was hit first, the judgement will go in favor of the shooter.

1.16.5. RACKING. The balls must be racked as tightly as possible, which means each ball should be touching its neighbor. Refrain from tapping object balls more than absolutely necessary; it is preferable to thoroughly brush the area of the rack to even out the cloth.

1.16.6. RESTORING A POSITION. If an object ball(s) is disturbed by a player and it does not effect the outcome of the shot, the other player has the option of calling upon the Tournament Director to restore the object ball(s) to its original position as soon as possible, or have the disturbed ball(s) left in its new position.

(Further Instructions for Tournament Play are Included in the Next Section "Instructions For Referees")

INSTRUCTIONS FOR REFEREES

2.1. TOURNAMENT OFFICIALS/REFEREES. Where these rules refer to a "referee," it should be noted that the referees' prerogatives and discretion also accrue to other tournament officials as appropriate.

2.2. REFEREE'S AUTHORITY. The referee will maintain order and enforce the rules of the game. He is the final judge in all matters of fact. The referee is in complete charge of the match he is officiating. He may, at his discretion, consult other tournament officials for rule interpretations, ball positions, etc. However, all matters of judgement are his and his alone; they cannot be appealed to higher tournament authority by players; only if the referee is in error on a rule or its application, may higher tournament authority overrule him.

2.3. REFEREE'S RESPONSIVENESS. The referee shall be totally responsive to players' inquiries regarding objective data, such as whether a ball will be in the rack, if a ball is in the kitchen, what the count is, how many points are needed for a victory, if a player is playing from safety, if a player or his opponent is on a foul, what rule would apply if a certain shot is made, etc. However, he must not offer or provide any subjective opinion that would affect play, such as whether a good hit can be made on a prospective shot, whether a combination is makeable, how the table seems to be playing, etc.

2.4. FINAL TOURNAMENT AUTHORITY. Though these rules attempt to cover the vast majority of situations that arise in competition, there still may be an occasional need for interpretation of the rules and their proper application under unusual circumstances. The Tournament Director or other official who assumes final responsibility for a tournament will make any such required decision (other than referee's judgement calls) at his discretion, and they shall be final.

2.5. WAGERING BY REFEREES. Referees are strictly prohibited from any wagering of any kind involving the games, players or tournament in any way. Any such wagering by a referee (or other tournament official) shall result in his immediate dismissal and the forfeiture of his entire financial compensation for the tournament.

2.6. BEFORE THE MATCH. Before the match, the referee will clean or have the table and balls cleaned if necessary. He will ensure that chalk, powder and mechanical bridges are available. He will mark or have the spots, the head string, the long string and the outer edge of the triangle marked with a pencil when required.

2.7. RACKING. The referee will rack the balls as tightly as possible, which means each ball should be touching its neighbors. Refrain from tapping balls more than necessary;

it is preferable to thoroughly brush the area of the rack to even out the cloth.When a referee is racking the balls for a game, neither player is allowed to examine the rack close up at anytime during or after the process.

2.8. CALLING SHOTS. For games of call-shot a player may shoot any ball he chooses, but before he shoots, must designate the called ball and *called pocket*. He need not indicate any detail such as *kisses, caroms, combinations,* or *cushions* (all of which are legal). Any additionally pocketed ball(s) on a legal stroke is counted in the shooter's favor.

If a referee incorrectly calls a shot, a player should correct him before completing the shot. If a mis-call does occur for any reason, the shot shall be credited if, in the referee's judgement, the player did legally execute the shot as intended.

2.9. CALLING FOULS. The referee will call fouls as soon as they occur and will inform the incoming player that he has ball in hand in games where the rule applies.

2.10. SPLIT HITS. When the referee observes that the cue ball strikes a legal object ball and a non-legal object ball at approximately the same instant, and it cannot be determined which ball was hit first, the judgement will go in favor of the shooter.

2.11. CLEARING POCKETS. On tables which do not have ball return systems, the referee will remove pocketed object balls from full or nearly full pockets. It is the player's responsibility to see that this duty is performed; he has no recourse if a ball rebounds from a full pocket.

2.12. CLEANING BALLS. During a game a player may ask the referee to clean one or more balls. The referee will clean any visibly soiled ball.

2.13. SPOTTING BALLS. To avoid any unnecessary guidance to a player when spotting balls, the referee should position each ball so that the number is facing upward.

2.14. SOLICITING INFORMATION. If the referee does not have a clear view of a possible foul, he may ask another tournament official, who may have had a better view of the incidence, for assistance in determining what occurred. The referee will then weigh all evidence as he sees fit and will make his decision.

2.15. INAPPROPRIATE USE OF EQUIPMENT. The referee should be alert for a player using equipment or accessory items for purposes or in a manner other than those for which the items were intended. Tournament officials should prevent these actions from occuring. Generally, no penalty is applied, because the referee or other tournament official intercedes prior to that point. However, should a player persist in activity counter to this (or any other) general rule after having been advised that the activity is not permissable, tournament officials may take action against him as appropriate under the provisions of "Unsportsmanlike Conduct."

2.16. WARNINGS WHICH ARE MANDATORY. The referee must warn a player who is about to commit a serious foul (such as three consecutive fouls, requesting coaching assistance, or failure to stop shooting after a foul has been called) whenever the referee has been given enough time to do so; otherwise, any foul is considered to be a standard foul (except as specially noted). In games where the rule applies the referee must inform a player who has had two consecutive fouls; otherwise, the player is considered to have had only one foul prior to the shot. The referee must inform a player when an object ball is touching a rail; otherwise, any contact on that ball is considered to have driven it to that rail. The referee should notify the player as soon as the corresponding situation arises and whenever enough time to warn was given by the shooter. A caution given just as a shot starts is not considered sufficient; the player as well must be given enough time to react.

2.17. RESTORING A POSITION. When it becomes necessary, the referee will restore disturbed balls to their original positions to the best of his ability. The referee may ask for information for this purpose if he is not sure of the original position.

2.18. OUTSIDE INTERFERENCE. When outside interference occurs during a shot that has an effect on the outcome of that shot, the referee will restore the balls to the positions they had before the shot, and the shot will be replayed. If the interference had no effect on the shot, the referee will restore the disturbed balls and play will continue. If the balls cannot be restored to their original positions, replay the game with the original player breaking.

2.19. ILLEGALLY CAUSING BALL TO MOVE. Any player who, in the referee's judgement, **intentionally** causes a ball to move by any illegal means (pushing on bed cloth, bumping or slapping table, etc.) will lose the game and/or match by forfeit. (Referee's judgement and discretion under "Unsportsmanlike Conduct.")

2.20. JUDGING DOUBLE HITS. When the distance between the cue ball and the object ball is less than the width of a chalk cube, special attention from the referee is required. In such a situation, unless the referee can positively determine a legal shot has been performed, the following guidance may apply: if the cue ball follows through the object ball more than 1/2 ball, it is a foul.

2.21. OUT OF HEAD STRING WARNING. When player has the *cue ball in hand behind the head string*, the referee shall warn him before he shoots if he has not placed it within the head string. If the player shoots on or outside the string after having been warned of the legal placement, the stroke is a foul. See specific game rules for penalty.

2.22. REMAINING IN PLAYER'S CHAIR. Players are to remain in the chair designated for their use while opponent is at the table. Should a player need to leave the playing area during matches, he must request and receive permission from the referee. The referee shall apply his good judgement to ensure that undue time is not being used or that a player is not abusing the privilege as a means of unsettling an opponent.

2.23. OUTSIDE ASSISTANCE PROHIBITED. Unless specifically permitted by the rules of a given tournament, players may not knowingly accept any form of playing advice during a match. A player may not engage in communication, either verbal or nonverbal, with persons other than the tournament officials or his opponent during play.

Should a player desire to so communicate, for example to obtain a beverage, get a piece of equipment, or other permissable reason, he should either communicate through a tournament official or with the approval and observance of the referee.

If the referee has reason to believe that a player knowingly solicited or accepted outside assistance in any manner regarding the play of a match, he shall take steps appropriate under the provisions of "Unsportsmanlike Conduct."

2.24. NON-PLAYER INTERFERENCE OR HARASSMENT. If a non-player either verbally or visually interferes with the players, the referee may request that he leave the playing area.

2.25. SLOW PLAY. (See Rule 1.11.)

2.26. PROTESTS. A player may request a rule interpretation or application from the referee or appropriate tournament authority. He must, however, make such a request or protest immediately, prior to any subsequent shot being taken, or it cannot be considered or honored.

All players must honor an opponent's request that play be halted if an official is to be summoned or if a referee is to check or verify a rule question with other officials. Failure to honor such requests may result in disqualification or forfeiture under the provisions of "Unsportsmanlike Conduct."

2.27. SUSPENDING PLAY. The referee has the authority to suspend play during protests by players and whenever he feels that conditions are unsuitable for play to continue. If a spectator is interfering with the game, play may be suspended until that spectator is removed from the area.

2.28. UNSPORTSMANLIKE CONDUCT. The referee has the right and obligation to ensure that no player engages in any activity which, in his judgement, is unsportsmanlike in nature, embarrassing, disruptive or detrimental to other players, tournament officials or hosts, or the sport in general. The referee or other officials shall have the right to penalize or disqualify, with or without warning, any player who conducts himself in an unsportsmanlike manner.

General Rules Of Pocket Billiards

These general rules apply to all pocket billiard games, UNLESS specifically noted to the contrary in the individual game rules.

To facilitate the use and understanding of these general rules, terms that may require definition are set in *italics* so that the reader may refer to the **Glossary of Billiard Terms** section for the exact meaning of the term.

3.1. TABLES, BALLS, EQUIPMENT. All games described in these rules are designed for tables, balls and equipment meeting the standards prescribed in the **BCA Equipment Specifications.**

3.2. RACKING THE BALLS. When racking the balls a triangle must be used, and the apex ball is to be spotted on the foot spot. All the balls must be lined up behind the apex ball and pressed together so that they all have contact with each other.

3.3. STRIKING CUE BALL. Legal shots require that the *cue ball* be struck only with the *cue tip*. Failure to meet this requirement is a *foul*.

3.4. FAILURE TO POCKET A BALL. If a player fails to pocket a ball on a legal shot, then the player's inning is over, and it is the opponent's turn at the table.

3.5. LAG FOR BREAK. The following procedure is used for the *lag* for the *opening break*. Each player should use balls of equal size and weight (preferably cue balls but, when not available, non-striped object balls). With the balls in hand behind the *head string*, one player to the left and one to the right of the *head spot*, the balls are shot simultaneously to the *foot cushion* and back to the head end of the table. The player whose ball is the closest to the innermost edge of the head cushion wins the lag. The lagged ball must contact the foot cushion at least once. Other cushion contacts are immaterial, except as prohibited below.

It is an automatic loss of the lag if: (1) the ball crosses into the opponent's half of the table, (2) the ball fails to contact the foot cushion, (3) the ball drops into a pocket, (4) the ball *jumps* the table, (5) the ball touches the long cushion, or (6) the ball rests within the corner pocket and past the nose of the head cushion. If both players violate automatic-loss lag rules, or if the referee is unable to determine which ball is closer, the lag is a tie and is replayed.

3.6. OPENING BREAK SHOT. The opening break shot is determined by either lag or *lot*. (The lag for break procedure is required for tournament and other formal competition.) The player winning the lag or lot has the choice of performing the opening break shot or assigning it to the opponent.

3.7. CUE BALL ON OPENING BREAK. The *opening break shot* is taken with *cue ball in hand behind the head string*. The object balls are positioned according to specific game rules. On the opening break, the game is considered to have commenced once the cue ball has been struck by the cue tip and crosses the head string.

3.8. CUE BALL IN HAND BEHIND THE HEAD STRING. This situation applies in specific games whereby a player's scratching is penalized by the incoming player having *cue ball in hand behind the headstring*. The incoming player may place the cue ball anywhere behind the headstring. If the player places the cue ball on or in front of the headstring and shoots, it is a foul. He may shoot at any object ball as long as the base of the object ball is on or past the headstring. He may not shoot at any ball the base of which is behind the headstring, unless he first shoots the cue ball past the headstring and then by hitting a rail causes the cue ball to come back behind the headstring and hit the object ball. The base of the ball (the point of the ball touching the table) determines whether it is within or out of the headstring. If the incoming player inadvertently places the cue ball in front of the headstring, it is a good gesture for his opponent to inform him before he shoots to avoid confusion.

When the cue ball is *in* hand behind the head string, it remains in hand (not in play) until the player drives the cue ball past the head string by striking it with his cue tip.

The cue ball may be ADJUSTED by the player's hand, cue, etc., so long as it remains in hand. Once the cue ball is in play per the above, it may not be impeded in any way by the player; to do so is to commit a foul.

3.9. POCKETED BALLS. A ball is considered as a pocketed ball if as a result of an otherwise legal shot, it drops off the bed of the table into the pocket and remains there. (A ball that drops out of a ball return system onto the floor is not to be construed as a ball that has not remained pocketed.) A ball that rebounds from a pocket back onto the table bed is not a pocketed ball.

3.10. POSITION OF BALLS. The position of a ball is judged by where its base (or center) rests.

3.11. FOOT ON FLOOR. It is a foul if a player shoots when at least one foot is not in contact with the floor. Foot attire must be normal in regard to size, shape and manner in which it is worn.

3.12. SHOOTING WITH BALLS IN MOTION. It is a foul if a player shoots while the cue ball or any object ball is in motion (a spinning ball is in motion).

3.13. COMPLETION OF STROKE. A stroke is not complete (and therefore is not counted) until all balls on the table have become motionless after the stroke (a spinning ball is in motion).

3.14. HEAD STRING DEFINED. The area behind the head string does not include the head string. Thus an object ball that is dead center on the head string is playable when specific game rules require that a player must shoot at a ball past the head string. Likewise, the cue ball when being put in play behind the head string (cue ball in hand behind the head string), may not be placed directly on the head string; it must be behind it.

3.15. GENERAL RULE, ALL FOULS. Though the penalties for fouls differ from game to game, the following apply to all fouls: (1) player's inning ends; (2) if on a stroke, the stroke is invalid and any pocketed balls are not counted to the shooter's credit; and (3) any ball(s) is respotted only if the rules of the specific game require it.

3.16. FAILURE TO CONTACT OBJECT BALL. It is a foul if on a stroke the cue ball fails to make contact with any legal object ball first. Playing away from a touching ball does not constitute having hit that ball.

3.17. LEGAL SHOT. Unless otherwise stated in a specific game rule, a player must cause the cue ball to contact a legal object ball and then (1) pocket an object ball, or (2) cause the cue ball or any object ball to contact a cushion. Failure to meet these requirements is a foul.

3.18. CUE BALL SCRATCH. It is a foul (scratch) if on a stroke, the cue ball is pocketed.

3.19. FOULS BY TOUCHING BALLS. It is a foul to strike, touch or in any way make contact with the cue ball in play or any object balls in play with anything (the body, clothing, chalk, mechanical bridge, cue shaft, etc.) EXCEPT the cue tip (while attached to the cue shaft), which may contact the cue ball in the execution of a legal shot. Whenever a referee is presiding over a match, any object ball moved during a standard foul must remain in its new position, and the incoming player does not have the option of restoration. (Also see Rule 1.16.)

3.20. FOUL BY PLACEMENT. Touching any object ball with the cue ball while it is in hand is a foul.

3.21. FOULS BY DOUBLE HITS. If the cue ball is touching the required object ball prior to the shot, the player may shoot towards it, providing that his cue stick strikes rather than pushes the cue ball. Attention must also be given so that any third ball which is close enough to interfere with the stroke is not moved with a cue, cue ball or object ball contact. If the cue ball is frozen in line with two or more frozen object balls, the player cannot shoot in a forward direction of the object balls. When the cue ball and object ball are close to each other, it is a foul when the tip of the cue remains in contact with the cue ball 1). after the cue ball has commenced its forward motion, or 2). when the cue ball makes contact with the object ball. (Also see Rule 2.20.)

3.22. PUSH SHOT FOULS. It is a foul if the cue ball is pushed by the cue tip, with contact being maintained for more than the momentary time commensurate with a stroked shot. (Such shots are usually referred to as *push shots*.) If, in the referee's judgement, the player lays the cue tip against the cue ball and then pushes on into the shot, maintaining contact beyond the normal momentary split-second, the stroke is a foul and must be so called.

3.23. PLAYER RESPONSIBILITY FOULS. The player is responsible for chalk, bridges, files and any other items or equipment he brings to, uses at, or causes to approximate the table. If he drops a piece of chalk, or knocks off a mechanical bridge head, as examples, he is guilty of a foul should such an object make contact with any ball in play (or the cue ball only if no referee is presiding over the match).

3.24. ILLEGAL JUMPING OF BALL. It is a foul if a player strikes the cue ball below center ("digs under" it) and intentionally causes it to rise off the bed of the table in an effort to clear an obstructing ball. Such jumping action may occasionally occur accidentally, and such "jumps" are not to be considered fouls on their face; they may still be ruled foul strokes, if for example, the ferrule or cue shaft makes contact with the cue ball in the course of the shot.

3.25. JUMP SHOTS. Unless otherwise stated in rules for a specific game it is legal to cause the cue ball to rise off the bed of the table by elevating the cue stick on the shot, and forcing the cue ball to rebound from the bed of the table. Any miscue when executing a jump shot is a foul.

3.26. BALLS JUMPED OFF TABLE. Balls coming to rest other than on the bed of the table after a stroke (on the cushion top, rail surface, floor, etc.) are considered jumped balls. Balls may bounce on the cushion tops and rails of the table in play without being jumped balls if they return to the bed of the table under their own power and without touching anything not a part of the table. The table shall consist of the permanent part of the table proper. (Balls that strike or touch anything not a part of the table, such as the light fixture, chalk on the rails and cushion tops, etc., shall be considered jumped balls even though they might return to the bed of the table after contacting items which are not parts of the table proper).

   In all pocket billiard games when a stroke results in the cue ball or any object ball being a jumped ball off the table, the stroke is a foul. All jumped object balls are spotted **(except in Nine Ball)** when all balls have stopped moving. See specific game rules for putting the cue ball in play after a jumped cue ball foul.

3.27. SPECIAL INTENTIONAL FOUL PENALTY. The cue ball in play shall not be intentionally struck with anything other than a cue's attached tip (such as the ferrule, shaft, etc.). While such contact is automatically a foul under the provisions of Rule 3.19., if the referee deems the contact to be intentional, he shall warn the player once during a match that a second violation during that match will result in the loss of the match by forfeiture. If a second violation does occur, the match must be forfeited.

3.28. ONE FOUL LIMIT. Unless specific game rules dictate otherwise, only one foul is assessed on a player in each inning; if different penalties can apply, the most severe penalty is the factor determining which foul is assessed.

3.29. BALLS MOVING SPONTANEOUSLY. If a ball shifts, settles, turns or otherwise moves "by itself," the ball shall remain in the position it assumed and play continues. A hanging ball that falls into a pocket "by itself" after being motionless for 5 seconds or longer shall be replaced as closely as possible to its position prior to falling, and play shall continue.

If an object ball drops into a pocket "by itself" as a player shoots at it, so that the cue ball passes over the spot the ball had been on, unable to hit it, the cue ball and object ball are to be replaced to their positions prior to the stroke, and the player must execute the shot again. Any other object balls disturbed on the stroke are also to be replaced to their original positions for the shot to be replayed.

3.30. SPOTTING BALLS. When specific game rules call for spotting balls, they shall be replaced on the table on the *long string* after the stroke is complete. A single ball is placed on the foot spot; if more than one ball is to be spotted, they are placed on the long string in ascending numerical order, beginning on the foot spot and advancing toward the foot rail.

When balls on or near the foot spot or long string interfere with the spotting of balls, the balls to be spotted are placed on the long string as close as possible to the foot spot without moving the interfering balls. Spotted balls are to be *placed as close as possible or frozen (at the referee's discretion)* to such interfering balls, except when the cue ball is interfering; balls to be spotted against the cue ball are placed as close as possible without being frozen.

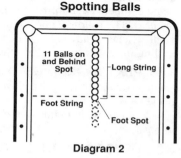

Spotting Balls

11 Balls on and Behind Spot

Long String

Foot String

Foot Spot

Diagram 2

If there is insufficient room on the long string between the foot spot and the foot rail cushion for balls that must be spotted, such balls are then placed on the extension of the long string "in front" of the foot spot (between the foot spot and the *center spot*), as near as possible to the foot spot and in the same numerical order as if they were spotted "behind" the foot spot (lowest numbered ball closest to the center of the table).

3.31. JAWED BALLS. If two or more balls are locked between the *jaws* or sides of the pocket, with one or more suspended in air, the referee shall inspect the balls in position and follow this procedure: he shall visually (or physically if he desires) project each ball directly downward from its locked position; any ball that in his judgement would fall in the pocket if so moved directly downward is a pocketed ball, while any ball that would come to rest on the bed of the table is not pocketed. The balls are then placed according to the referee's assessment, and play continues according to specific game rules as if no locking or jawing of balls had occurred.

3.32. ADDITIONAL POCKETED BALLS. If a player completes a legal, scoring stroke on which an object ball or balls in addition to the intended, called, required or designated ball or balls also drop, such additional balls shall be counted, credited and scored in accord with the scoring rules for the particular game.

3.33. NON-PLAYER INTERFERENCE. If the balls are moved (or a player bumped such that play is directly affected) by a non-player during the match, the balls shall be replaced as near as possible to their original positions immediately prior to the incident, and play shall resume with no penalty on the player affected. If the match is officiated, the referee shall replace the balls. This rule shall also apply to "act of God" interference, such as earthquake, hurricane, light fixture falling, power failure, etc. If the balls cannot be restored to their original positions, replay the game with the original player breaking. This rule is not applicable to 14.1 Continuous where the game consists of successive racks: the rack in progress will be discontinued and a completely new rack will be started with the requirements of the normal opening break (players lag for break). Scoring of points is to be resumed at the score as it stood at the moment of game disruption.

3.34. BREAKING SUBSEQUENT RACKS. When *short-rack games* are being competed in a format requiring sets or races, winner of each game breaks the next. The following are common options that may be designated by tournament officials in advance: (1) Players alternate break. (2) Loser breaks. (3) Player trailing in games score breaks the next game.

3.35. PLAY BY INNINGS. During the course of play, players alternate turns (innings) at the table, with a player's inning ending when he either fails to legally pocket a ball, or fouls.

When an inning ends free of a foul, the incoming player accepts the table in position.

3.36. OBJECT BALL FROZEN TO CUSHION OR CUE BALL. This rule applies to any shot where the cue ball's first contact with a ball is with one that is frozen to a cushion or to the cue ball itself. After the cue ball makes contact with the frozen object ball, the shot must result in either (1) a ball being pocketed, or (2) the cue ball contacting a cushion, or (3) the frozen ball being caused to contact a cushion (not merely rebounding from the cushion it was frozen to), or (4) another object ball being caused to contact a cushion to which it was not already in contact with. Failure to satisfy one of those four requirements is a foul. (Note: 14.1 and other games specify additional requirements and applications of this rule; see specific game rules.)

An object ball is not considered frozen to a rail unless it is examined and announced as such by either the referee or one of the players prior to that object ball being involved in a shot

3.37. PLAYING FROM BEHIND THE STRING. When a player has the cue ball in hand behind the string (in the kitchen), he must drive the cue ball to a point outside the kitchen before it contacts either a cushion or an object ball. Failure to do so is either a foul, or at opponent's option, offending player can be required to replay the shot again with the balls restored to their positions prior to the shot (and with no foul penalty imposed).

Exception: if an object ball lies on or outside the head string (and is thus playable) but so close that the cue ball contacts it before the cue ball is out of the kitchen, the ball can be legally played.

If, with cue ball in hand behind the headstring and while the shooter is attempting a legitimate shot, the cue ball accidentally hits a ball behind the head string, and the cue ball crosses the line, it is a foul. If with cue ball in hand behind the head string, the shooter causes the cue ball to accidentally hit an object ball, and the cue ball does not cross the headstring, the following applies: the incoming player has the option of calling a foul and having cue ball in hand, or having the balls returned to their original position, and having the offending player replay the shot.

If a player under the same conditions intentionally causes the cue ball to contact an object ball behind the headstring, it is unsportsmanlike conduct.

3.38. CUE BALL FOUL. During cue ball in hand placement, if a player touches the cue ball with the chalked surface of his cue tip, he has fouled.

3.39. INTERFERENCE. If the nonshooting player distracts his opponent or interferes with his play, he has fouled. If a player shoots out of turn, or moves any ball except during his inning, it is considered to be interference.

3.40. DEVICES. Players are not allowed to use a ball, the triangle or any other width-measuring device to see if the cue ball or an object ball would travel through a gap, etc. Only the cue may be used as an aid to judge gaps, etc., so long as the cue is held by the hand. To do so otherwise is a foul and unsportsmanlike conduct.

TOURNAMENT POCKET BILLIARD GAMES

— EIGHT BALL —

Except when clearly contradicted by these additional rules,
the **General Rules of Pocket Billiards** apply.

4.1. OBJECT OF THE GAME: Eight Ball is a *call shot* game played with a cue ball and fifteen object balls, numbered 1 through 15. One player must pocket balls of the group numbered 1 through 7 (solid colors), while the other player has 9 thru 15 (stripes). THE PLAYER POCKETING HIS GROUP FIRST AND THEN LEGALLY POCKETING THE 8-BALL WINS THE GAME.

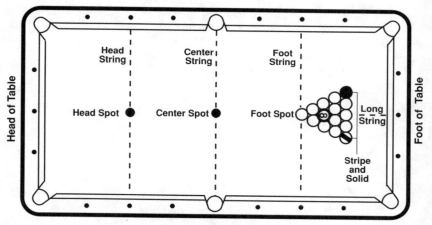

Diagram 3

4.2. CALL SHOT: In Call Shot, obvious balls and pockets do not have to be indicated. It is the opponent's right to ask which ball and pocket if he is unsure of the shot. Banks and combinations are not considered obvious and both the object ball and the pocket must be called. When calling the shot, it is NEVER necessary to indicate details such as the number of *cushions, banks, kisses, caroms,* etc. Any balls pocketed on a foul remain pocketed, regardless of whether they belong to the shooter or the opponent.

The opening break is not a "called shot." Any player performing a break shot in 8-Ball may continue to shoot his next shot so long as he has legally pocketed any object ball on the break.

4.3. RACKING THE BALLS: The balls are *racked* in a triangle at the foot of the table with the 8-ball in the center of the triangle, the first ball of the rack on the footspot, a stripe ball in one corner of the rack and a solid ball in the other corner.

4.4. ALTERNATING BREAK: Winner of the lag has the option to *break*. During individual competition, players will alternate breaking on each subsequent game.

4.5. LEGAL BREAK SHOT: (Defined) To execute a legal break, the breaker (with the cue ball behind the headstring) must either (1) pocket a ball, or (2) drive at least four numbered balls to the rail. If he fails to make a legal break, it is a foul, and the incoming player has the option of (1) accepting the table in position and shooting, or (2) having the balls reracked and having the option to shoot the opening break himself. It is *not* necessary to hit the apex ball (the ball that is on the foot spot) to initiate a legal break in Eight Ball.

4.6. SCRATCH ON A LEGAL BREAK: If a player *scratches* on a legal break shot, (1) all balls pocketed remain pocketed (exception, the 8-ball: see rule 4.7), (2) it is a foul, (3) the table is open. PLEASE NOTE: Incoming player has cue ball in hand behind the head string and may not shoot an object ball that is behind the head string, unless he first shoots the cue ball past the headstring and causes the cue ball to come back behind the headstring and hit the object ball.

4.7. 8-BALL POCKETED ON THE BREAK: If the 8-ball is pocketed on the break, the breaker may ask for a re-rack or have the 8-ball spotted and continue shooting. If the breaker scratches while pocketing the 8-ball on the break, the incoming player has the option of a re-rack or having the 8-ball spotted and begin shooting with ball in hand behind the headstring.

4.8. OPEN TABLE: (Defined) The table is "open" when the choice of groups (stripes or solids) has not yet been determined. When the table is open, it is legal to hit a solid first to make a stripe or vice-versa. Note: The table is always open immediately after the break shot. When the table is open it is legal to hit any solid or stripe or the 8-ball first in the process of pocketing the called stripe or solid. On an open table, all illegally pocketed balls remain pocketed.

4.9. CHOICE OF GROUP: The choice of stripes or solids is not determined on the break even if balls are made from only one or both groups. THE TABLE IS ALWAYS OPEN IMMEDIATELY AFTER THE BREAK SHOT. The choice of group is determined only when a player legally pockets a called object ball after the break shot.

4.10. LEGAL SHOT: (Defined) On all shots (except on the break and when the table is *open*), the shooter must hit one of his group of balls first and (1) pocket an object ball, or (2) cause the cue ball or any object ball to contact a *rail*.

PLEASE NOTE: It is permissable for the shooter to bank the cue ball off a rail before contacting his object ball; however, after contact with his object ball, an object ball must be pocketed, OR the cue ball or any object ball must contact a rail.

4.11. "SAFETY" SHOT: For tactical reasons a player may choose to pocket an obvious object ball and also discontinue his turn at the table by declaring "safety" in advance. A safety shot is defined as a legal shot. If the shooting player intends to play safe by pocketing an obvious object ball, then prior to the shot, he must declare a "safety" to his opponent. If this is NOT done, and one of the shooter's object balls is pocketed, the shooter will be required to shoot again. Any ball pocketed on a safety shot remains pocketed.

4.12. SCORING: A player is entitled to continue shooting until he fails to legally pocket a ball of his group. After a player has legally pocketed all of his group of balls, he shoots to pocket the 8-ball.

4.13. FOUL PENALTY: Opposing player gets *cue ball in hand*. This means that the player can place the cue ball anywhere on the table (does not have to be behind the headstring except on opening break). This rule prevents a player from making intentional fouls which would put his opponent at a disadvantage. With "cue ball in hand," the player may position the cue ball on the table by hand (more than once if necessary). After placing the cue ball, the shaft and *ferrule* of the cue stick (not the tip) may also be used for positioning the cue ball for shooting.

4.14. COMBINATION SHOTS: Combination shots are allowed; however, the 8-ball cannot be used as a first ball in the combination except when the table is open.

4.15. ILLEGALLY POCKETED BALLS: An object ball is considered to be illegally pocketed when (1) that object ball is pocketed on the same shot a foul is committed, or (2) the called ball did not go in the designated pocket, or (3) a safety is called prior to the shot. Illegally pocketed balls remain pocketed.

4.16. OBJECT BALLS JUMPED OFF THE TABLE: If any object ball is jumped off the table, it is a foul and loss of turn, unless it is the 8-ball, which is a loss of game. Any jumped object balls are spotted in numerical order according to General Rules for spotting balls.

4.17. PLAYING THE 8-BALL: When shooting at the 8-ball, a scratch or foul is not loss of game if the 8-ball is not pocketed or jumped from the table. Incoming player has cue ball in hand.

4.18. LOSS OF GAME: A player loses the game if he commits any of the following infractions:

   a. Fouls when pocketing the 8-ball (exception: see 8-BALL POCKETED ON THE BREAK).
   b. Pockets the 8-ball on the same stroke as the last of his group of balls.
   c. Jumps the 8-ball off the table at any time.
   d. Pockets the 8-ball in a pocket other than the one designated.
   e. Pockets the 8-ball when it is not the legal object ball.

4.19. STALEMATED GAME: If in 3 consecutive turns at the table by each player (6 turns total), they purposely foul or scratch and both players agree that attempting to pocket or move an object ball will result in immediate loss of game, then the game will be considered a stalemate. The balls will then be re-racked and the breaker of the stalemated game will break again. PLEASE NOTE: Three consecutive fouls by one player is not a loss of game.

NINE BALL

[Professional and World Rules]

Except when clearly contradicted by these additional rules,
the **General Rules of Pocket Billiards** apply.

5.1 OBJECT OF THE GAME. Nine Ball is played with nine object balls numbered one through nine and a cue ball. On each shot the first ball the cue ball contacts must be the lowest-numbered ball on the table, but the balls need not be pocketed in order. If a player pockets any ball on a legal shot, he remains at the table for another shot, and continues until he misses, fouls, or wins the game by pocketing the 9-ball. After a miss, the incoming player must shoot from the position left by the previous player, but after any foul the incoming player may start with the cue ball anywhere on the table. Players are not required to call any shot. A match ends when one of the players has won the required number of games.

5.2. RACKING THE BALLS. The object balls are racked in a diamond shape, with the one ball at the top of the diamond and on the foot spot, the nine ball in the center of the diamond, and the other balls in random order, racked as tightly as possible. The game begins with cue ball in hand behind the head string.

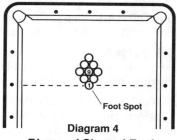

Diagram 4
Diamond Shaped Rack
1-Ball must be on the foot spot.
9-Ball must be in the center of the rack.

5.3. LEGAL BREAK SHOT. The rules governing the break shot are the same as for other shots except:

a. The breaker must strike the 1-ball first and either pocket a ball or drive at least four numbered balls to the rail.

b. If the cue ball is pocketed or driven off the table, or the requirements of the opening break are not met, it is a foul, and the incoming player has cue ball in hand anywhere on the table.

c. If on the break shot, the breaker causes an object ball to jump off the table, it is a foul and the incoming player has cue ball in hand anywhere on the table. The object ball is not respotted.

5.4. CONTINUING PLAY. On the shot immediately following a legal break, the shooter may play a "push out." (See Rule 5.5.). If the breaker pockets one or more balls on a legal break, he continues to shoot until he misses, fouls, or wins the game. If the player misses or fouls, the other player begins his inning and shoots until he misses, fouls, or wins. The game ends when the nine ball is pocketed on a legal shot, or the game is forfeited for a serious infraction of the rules.

5.5. PUSH OUT. The player who shoots the shot immediately after a legal break may play a *push out* in an attempt to move the cue ball into a better position for the option that follows. On a push out, the cue ball is not required to contact any object ball nor any rail, but all other foul rules still apply. The player must announce his intention of playing a push out before the shot, or the shot is considered to be a normal shot. Any ball pocketed on a push out does not count and remains pocketed. Following a legal push out, the incoming player is permitted to shoot from that position or to pass the shot back to the player who pushed out. A push out is not considered to be a foul as long as no rule (except rules 5.7. and 5.8.) is violated. An illegal push out is penalized according to the type of foul committed.

5.6. FOULS. When a player commits a foul, he must relinquish his run at the table and no balls pocketed on the foul shot are spotted. The incoming player is awarded ball in hand; prior to his first shot he may place the cue ball anywhere on the table. If a player commits several fouls on one shot, they are counted as only one foul.

5.7. BAD HIT. If the first object ball contacted by the cue ball is not the lowest-numbered ball on the table, the shot is foul.

5.8. NO RAIL. If no object ball is pocketed, failure to drive the cue ball or some object ball to a rail after the cue ball contacts the object ball on is a foul.

5.9. IN HAND. When the cue ball is in hand, the player may place the cue ball anywhere on the bed of the table, except in contact with an object ball. He may continue to adjust the position of the cue ball until he takes a shot.

5.10. OBJECT BALLS JUMPED OFF THE TABLE. An unpocketed ball is considered to be driven off the table if it comes to rest other than on the bed of the table. It is a foul to drive an object ball off the table. The jumped object ball(s) is not spotted and play continues.

5.11. THREE CONSECUTIVE FOULS. If a player fouls three consecutive times on three successive shots without making an intervening legal shot, he loses the game. The three fouls must occur in one game. The warning must be given between the second and third fouls.

A player's inning begins when it is legal for him to take a shot and ends at the end of a shot on which he misses, fouls or wins, or when he fouls between shots.

5.12. END OF GAME. A game starts as soon as the cue ball crosses over the head string on the opening break. The 1-ball must be legally contacted on the break shot. The game ends at the end of a legal shot which pockets the 9-ball; or when a player forfeits the game as the result of a foul.

14.1 CONTINUOUS
[Professional and World Rules]
Except when clearly contradicted by these additional rules,
the **General Rules of Pocket Billiards** apply.

6.1. OBJECT OF THE GAME. 14.1 is a nomination game. The player must nominate a ball and a pocket. The player is awarded one point for every correctly nominated and pocketed ball on a legal stroke, and is allowed to continue his turn until he either fails to pocket a nominated ball or commits a foul. The player can pocket the first 14 balls, but before he can continue his turn by shooting at the 15th (and last remaining) ball on the table, the 14 pocketed balls are racked as before, except with the apex space vacant. The player then attempts to pocket the 15th ball in a manner so that the racked balls are disturbed and he can continue his run.

The player who scores the pre-determined point total for a game (usually 150 in major tournament play or any agreed upon total in casual play) prior to his opponent, wins the game.

6.2. PLAYERS. 2, or 2 teams.

6.3. BALLS USED. Standard set of object balls numbered 1-15, plus *cue ball*.

6.4. THE RACK. Standard *triangle* rack with the apex ball on the *foot spot*, 1-ball on the racker's right corner, 5-ball on left corner. Other balls are placed at random and must touch their neighbors.

6.5. SCORING. Any ball legally pocketed counts one point for the shooter.

6.6. OPENING BREAK. Starting player must either (1) designate a ball and a pocket into which that ball will be pocketed and accomplish the shot, or (2) cause the cue ball to contact a ball and then a cushion, plus cause two object balls to contact a cushion. Failure to meet at least one of the above requirements is a *breaking violation*. Offender's score is assessed a two point penalty for each breaking violation. In addition, the opponent has the choice of (1) accepting the *table in position*, or (2) having the balls reracked and requiring the offending player to repeat the opening break. That choice continues until the opening break is not a breaking violation, or until the opponent accepts the table in position. The three *successive fouls* rule does not apply to breaking violations.

If the starting player scratches on a legal opening break, he is charged with a foul and assessed a one point penalty, which applies toward the "Successive Fouls Penalties." The incoming player is awarded *cue ball in hand behind the head string*, with object balls in position.

6.7. RULES OF PLAY.

1. A legally pocketed ball entitles a shooter to continue at the table until he fails to legally pocket a *called ball* on a shot. A player may shoot any ball he chooses, but before he shoots, must designate the called ball and *called pocket*. He need not indicate any detail such as *kisses, caroms, combinations,* or *cushions* (all of

which are legal). Any additionally pocketed ball(s) on a legal stroke is scored as one point for the shooter.

2. On all shots, a player must cause the cue ball to contact an object ball and then (1) pocket an object ball, or (2) cause the cue ball or any object ball to contact a cushion. Failure to meet these requirements is a foul.

When an object ball is not *frozen* to a cushion, but is within a ball's width of a cushion (referee to determine by measurement if necessary), a player is permitted only two legal safeties on that ball using only the near rail. If such safety play is employed, that object ball is then considered frozen to the rail on the player's next inning. The **General Rules of Pocket Billiards** "Frozen Balls" requirements apply if the player chooses to make his first cue ball contact with that object ball on his third shot.

(**Note:** If a player has committed a foul on his previous shot effort before playing this ball, he is allowed only one legal safety on the ball using the near rail. He must then meet the requirements of the "Frozen Ball" rule on his next shot. If he has committed two consecutive fouls, he must immediately meet the requirements of the "Frozen Ball" rule when playing this object ball. If such player fails to meet the requirements of the "Frozen Ball" rule, he is considered to have committed a third successive foul and the appropriate point penalty is assessed as well as one point for each of the previous fouls. All fifteen balls are then reracked and the player committing the infraction is required to break as at the beginning of the game.)

3. When the fourteenth ball of a rack is pocketed, play stops momentarily with the fifteenth ball remaining in position on the table; the fourteen pocketed balls are then racked (with the space at the foot spot vacant in the triangle). Player then continues, normally pocketing the fifteenth (or "break" ball) in such manner as to have the cue ball carom into the rack and spread the balls to facilitate the continuance of his run. However, player is not compelled to shoot the fifteenth ball; he may shoot any ball he desires.

See Diagram 5 if the fifteenth ball is pocketed on the same stroke as the fourteenth ball.

4. A player may call a *safety* rather than an object ball (for defensive purposes). Safety play is legal, but must comply with all applicable rules. Player's inning ends when a safety is played, and pocketed balls are not scored. Any object ball pocketed on a called safety is spotted.

5. A player may not catch, touch, or in any way interfere with a ball as it travels toward a pocket or the rack area on a shot (to include catching a ball as it enters a pocket by having a hand in the pocket). If he does, he is charged with a special "deliberate foul" and is penalized one point for the foul and an additional fifteen point penalty, for a total of sixteen points. The incoming player then has choice of (1) accepting the *table in position* with the cue ball in hand behind the head string, or (2) having all fifteen balls reracked and requiring the offending player to shoot under the requirements of the opening break.

6. If the fifteenth (unpocketed) ball of a rack and/or the cue ball interferes with the triangle being lowered straight down into position for racking, refer to the

diagram , which indicates the proper manner of relocating balls. (The lined out boxes are those situations in which there is no interference, both balls remain in position.)

14.1– What to do if:

15th Ball Lies \ Cue Ball Lies	IN THE RACK	NOT IN THE RACK AND NOT ON HEAD SPOT*	ON HEAD SPOT*
IN THE RACK	15th Ball: foot spot. Cue Ball: in kitchen	15th Ball: head spot. Cue Ball: in position	15th Ball: center spot. Cue Ball: in position.
POCKETED	15th Ball: foot spot. Cue Ball: in kitchen.	15th Ball: foot spot. Cue Ball: in position	15th Ball: foot spot. Cue Ball: in position.
IN KITCHEN BUT NO ON HEAD SPOT*	15th Ball: in position. Cue Ball: head spot.		
NOT IN KITCHEN & NOT IN THE RACK	15th Ball: in position. Cue Ball: in kitchen.		
ON HEAD SPOT*	15th Ball: in position. Cue Ball: center spot.		*On head spot means to interfere with spotting a ball on the head spot

Diagram 5

7. When a player has the cue ball in hand behind the head string (as after a scratch) and all object balls are behind the head string, the object ball nearest the head string may be spotted at his request. If two or more balls are an equal distance from the head string, the player may designate which of the equidistant balls he desires to have spotted.

6.8. ILLEGALLY POCKETED BALLS. All spotted. No penalty.

6.9. OBJECT BALLS JUMPED OFF THE TABLE. The stroke is a foul. Any jumped ball(s) is spotted after the balls come to rest.

6.10. CUE BALL AFTER JUMPING OFF THE TABLE OR SCRATCH.
Incoming player has cue ball in hand behind the head string, unless the provision of Rule of Play 6.7.2., 6.7.5. or 6.12." (below) apply to the offender's foul and dictate alternate choices or procedures.

6.11. PENALTIES FOR FOULS. One point deducted for each foul; NOTE: more severe penalties for deliberate fouls (Rule of Play 6.7.5.) and third "Successive Fouls" (6.12. below). Incoming player accepts cue ball in position unless foul was a jumped cue ball, pocket scratch, deliberate foul (Rule of Play 6.7.5.) or third successive foul.

6.12. SUCCESSIVE FOUL PENALTIES. When a player commits a foul, he is penalized one point (or more as appropriate) and a notation is made and posted by the scorer that he is "on a foul." The player remains "on a foul" until his next shot attempt, at which time he may remove the foul by successfully pocketing a called ball, or completing a legal safety. If he fails to meet these requirements on his next turn at the table, he is penalized one point. The notation is changed to "on two fouls." If he fails to meet the requirements of successfully pocketing a called ball or completing a legal safety on his third consecutive turn at the table, a penalty of fifteen points is assessed.

The commission of a third successive foul automatically clears the offender's record of fouls.

All balls are then reracked and the player committing the infraction is required to break as at the beginning of the game. Rules for the opening break apply.

It should be emphasized that successive fouls must be committed in successive turns (or playing attempts), **not** merely in successive innings. For example, if a player ends inning 6 with a foul, steps to the table for inning 7 and fouls (he is "on two fouls"), and then starts inning 8 with a legally pocketed ball before scratching on his second shot attempt of the inning, he has not committed three successive fouls, even though there were fouls in three successive innings. As soon as he legally pocketed the ball to start inning 8, he cleared the two fouls. He is, of course, "on one foul" when he plays the first stroke attempt of inning 9.

6.13. SCORING NOTE. The deduction of penalty points can result in negative scores. A running score can read "minus one," "minus two," "minus fifteen," etc. (A player can win a game with a score of 150 while his opponent has scored but two fouls. The final score would read 150 to -2.)

If a player fouls on a shot that has not pocketed a ball, the point penalty is deducted from his score at the end of the previous inning. If a player fouls and pockets a ball on the same shot, that ball is spotted (not scored) and the point penalty is deducted from his score at the end of the previous inning.

SEVEN BALL

Except when clearly contradicted by these additional rules,
the **General Rules of Pocket Billiards** apply.

TYPE OF GAME: Seven Ball is a new, speedy rotational game designed to meet the time requirements of television. Averaging only about three minutes per game because contestants shoot at the same seven object balls, it permits players to show skills in making *combination* and *carom* shots, defensive shots and placement. At the same time, it is attractive to players of moderate skills, and readily adapts to handicapping by limiting the number of pockets in which the better contestant can legally pocket the game-winning 7-ball. Any nationwide commercial use of this game (patent pending) should be cleared in advance with Big Fights, Inc., 9 East 40th St., New York, New York 10016.

PLAYERS: 2, or 2 teams.

BALLS USED: Object balls numbered 1-7, plus *cue ball.*

THE RACK: A special circular rack has been designed for this game. A standard *diamond* rack (as used in **Nine Ball**) may also be used by turning it sideways.

The balls are racked in a circle on the *foot spot*, with the 1-ball at the apex (12 o'clock) and the balls increasing numerically 1-6 (clockwise in a circle) with the 7-ball in the middle of the circle. (See Diagram 6.)

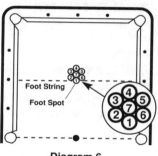

Seven Ball Rack

Diagram 6

OBJECT OF THE GAME: To legally pocket the 7-ball.

SCORING: The balls have no point value. The player legally pocketing the 7-ball is credited with a game won.

OPENING BREAK: The starting player must (1) make an *open break*, or (2) legally pocket an object ball. If he fails to do so, incoming player has choice of foul Penalty 1, or having the balls reracked and shooting the opening break shot himself. In subsequent games players alternate the break shot.

RULES OF PLAY:

1. A legal shot requires that the cue ball's first contact be with the lowest-numbered ball on the table. A player must then (1) pocket a ball, or (2) cause the cue ball or any object ball to contact a *cushion*. Failure to meet these requirements is a *foul* and Penalty for Fouls 2 applies.

2. A legally pocketed ball entitles a shooter to remain at the table until he fails to pocket a ball on a legal shot.

3. After a legal opening break, opponent chooses which side of the table (any of the three pockets on one side) into which he will pocket the 7-ball. Balls 1-6 may be pocketed on either side of the table.

4. Pocketing the 7-ball on a fair opening break wins the game.

5. Any violation of **General Rules** results in Penalty for Fouls 2.

LOSS OF GAME: A player loses the game if he commits any of the following infractions: (a) pockets the 7-ball in a non-assigned pocket after the break, (b) scratches when the 7-ball is his legal object ball, (c) pockets the 7 ball on an illegal shot; (d) misses when the 7-ball is his object ball (optional–an alternative is to assess Foul Penalty 2); (e) commits three successive fouls.

ILLEGALLY POCKETED OBJECT BALLS: All *spotted*; Penalty for Fouls 2 applies. (Optional for coin-operated tables: all balls remain pocketed; Penalty for Fouls 2 applies.)

OBJECT BALLS JUMPED OFF THE TABLE: All spotted. The stroke is a foul, and Penalty for Fouls 2 applies.

CUE BALL AFTER JUMP OR SCRATCH: Incoming player has cue ball in hand.

PENALTY FOR FOULS: No point penalty. (1) Incoming player has *cue ball in hand behind the head string* and object balls in position, but if the lowest numbered object ball is also behind head string it must be spotted. (2) *Cue ball in hand* anywhere on the table.

VARIATION: Players of unequal ability may be handicapped by assigning them more or less pockets in which they can play the 7-ball. It is suggested that more skilled players shoot the 7-ball into the side pocket on their side of the table. Players may also agree that the 7-ball can be pocketed anywhere on table.

—————— TEN BALL ——————

Except when clearly contradicted by these additional rules,
the **General Rules of Pocket Billiards** apply.

TYPE OF GAME: Ten Ball is a variation of **Rotation** in which a rack of just ten object balls is employed. As you will discern from the following rules, it is virtually the same game as **Nine Ball**, but with the extra ball adding both additional difficulty and generally fewer balls being pocketed on the opening break (particularly the ten-, or game-ball). Still, accomplished players turn it into a fast, action packed game!

PLAYERS: 2 or more, though 2, 3, or 4 is generally preferred.

BALLS USED: *Object balls* 1-10, plus *cue ball*.

THE RACK: *Triangle rack* truncated by removal of the rear row of balls (rows 1-2-3-4) with the 1-ball on the *foot spot*, and the 10-ball in the center of the row-of-3; other balls may be placed entirely at random.

OBJECT OF THE GAME: To legally pocket the 10-ball.

SCORING: The balls have no point value. The player legally pocketing the 10-ball is credited with a game won.

OPENING BREAK: The starting player must either (1) make an *open break*, or (2) legally pocket an object ball. If he fails to do so, incoming player has choice of (1)*cue ball in hand behind the head string* and object balls in position, or (2) having the balls reracked and shooting the opening break shot himself.

RULES OF PLAY:

1. A legal shot requires that the cue ball's first contact with a ball is with the lowest-numbered ball on the table. AND THEN either (1) pocket a ball, or (2) cause the cue ball or any object ball to contact a cushion. Failure to meet this requirement is a foul.

2. A legally pocketed ball entitles shooter to remain at the table until he fails to pocket a ball on a legal shot.

3. When a player legally pockets a ball, he must shoot again. He may not call a *safety* and spot a legally pocketed ball.

4. It is loss of game if a player commits three successive fouls.

ILLEGALLY POCKETED BALLS: All spotted, no penalty. (Common option, coin-op play: None spotted except the game-ball, no penalty.)

OBJECT BALLS JUMPED OFF THE TABLE: All spotted. The stroke is a foul, and the incoming player has cue ball in hand, except after the break shot.

CUE BALL AFTER JUMPING OFF THE TABLE OR SCRATCH: Incoming player has *cue ball in hand*, except after the break shot.

PENALTY FOR FOULS: Incoming player is awarded *cue ball in hand*. (Note: Rule of Play 4 calls for loss of game if the foul is a 3rd successive one.)

ROTATION

Except when clearly contradicted by these additional rules,
the **General Rules of Pocket Billiards** apply.

Rotation requires that the cue ball must contact the lowest-numbered object ball first on each shot; any ball pocketed on a legal shot counts. It is not necessary to call balls or pockets. It is a formidable test of a player's imagination, shot-making and repertoire. Few games require more exacting position play.

PLAYERS: 2 or more.

BALLS USED: Standard set of object balls 1-15, plus *cue ball*.

THE RACK: Standard *triangle* rack with the 1-ball on the foot spot, 2-ball on the right rear corner, 3-ball on the left rear corner, and 15-ball in the center. All other balls placed entirely at random.

OBJECT OF THE GAME: To score balls of greater total point value than opponent(s).

SCORING: Each legally pocketed object ball has a point value equal to its number. When a player's point total mathematically eliminates an opponent(s) from outscoring him (61 points in a two-player game), the game is ended. If two or more players tie for highest point total after all fifteen object balls have been pocketed, the tied player who legally pocketed the last object ball is credited with an extra tie-breaking point and wins the game.

OPENING BREAK: The starting player must (1) make an *open break*, or (2) legally pocket an object ball. If he fails to do so, the incoming player has the choice of (1) shooting with *cue ball in hand behind the head string* and object balls in position, or (2) having the balls reracked and shooting the opening break shot himself.

RULES OF PLAY:

1. A legal shot requires that the cue ball's first contact be with the lowest-numbered ball on the table. A player must then (1) pocket a ball, or (2) cause the cue ball or any object ball to contact a cushion. Failure is a foul.

2. A legally pocketed ball entitles a shooter to remain at the table until he fails to pocket a ball on a legal shot. If necessary, a player is permitted only two legal safeties played by merely hitting that object ball (only) to the near cushion.

3. When a player legally pockets a ball, he must shoot again. He may not call a *safety* and spot a legally pocketed object ball.

4. When a player has the cue ball in hand behind the head string (as after a scratch) and the legal object ball is also behind the headstring, the object ball may be spotted on the foot spot at his request.

5. It is a loss of game if a player commits three *successive fouls*. In more than a two player game, balls pocketed by disqualified players remain off the table.

ILLEGALLY POCKETED BALLS: All spotted.

OBJECT BALLS JUMPED OFF THE TABLE: All spotted. The stroke is a foul, and the penalty for fouls is followed.

CUE BALL AFTER JUMPING OFF THE TABLE OR SCRATCH: Incoming player has cue ball in hand behind the head string.

PENALTY FOR FOULS: No point penalty. Incoming player has the option of (1) accepting the balls in position, or (2) requiring offending player to shoot again with the table in position (if cue ball is in hand behind the string it is so for either player). Rule of Play 5 takes precedence in the case of a third consecutive foul.

BANK POOL

Except when clearly contradicted by these additional rules,
the **General Rules of Pocket Billiards** apply.

TYPE OF GAME: In **Bank Pool**, each shot must be a *bank* of an object ball into at least one cushion before the ball is pocketed. "Straight-in" shots are not legal. It is by definition a demanding game, and fascinating to observe, particularly when the players are accomplished at the art of banking.

PLAYERS: 2, 3, 4 or 5 players, though 2 players are generally preferred.

BALLS USED: Standard set of object balls 1-15, plus *cue ball*.

THE RACK: Standard *triangle* rack; balls placed entirely at random.

OBJECT OF THE GAME: To score a greater number of balls than opponent(s).

SCORING: Each legally pocketed object ball is scored as one ball. In two-player games, the first player to score eight balls wins. In three-player games, the first player to score five balls wins. In four-player games, the first player to score four balls wins. In five-player games, the first scored ball (though credited to the shooter) is immediately *spotted*, and the player continues to shoot; the first player to score four balls wins.

OPENING BREAK: Starting player must make an *open break*. If he fails to do so, incoming player has choice of (1) accepting the table in position and shooting, or (2) having the balls reracked and shooting the opening break shot himself.

No balls may be scored on the *opening break*. If any balls are pocketed on a legal opening break shot, they are spotted and the breaker continues shooting.

RULES OF PLAY:

1. A legally pocketed ball entitles shooter to remain at the table until he fails to legally pocket a ball. Player may shoot any object ball, but must designate which ball, pocket and the cushion(s) that ball will contact. A legally pocketed ball must be driven into at least one cushion and rebounded into the *called pocket*.

2. A legally pocketed ball must be "cleanly" banked (i.e., no *kisses*, no *combinations*, or *caroms* involving the *object ball* are permitted). The cue ball may contact the object ball only once on a stroke.

3. On a legal scoring stroke, only the object ball is credited to the shooter. Any other balls pocketed on the same stroke do not count for the shooter, and may be subject to special spotting provisions regarding "Illegally Pocketed Balls."

4. When a player has the *cue ball in hand behind the head string* (as after a scratch) and all object balls are also behind the head string, the object ball nearest the head string may be spotted on the foot spot at his request. If two or more balls are an equal distance from the head string, the player may also designate which of the balls he desires to be spotted.

5. Cushion impact shall mean clear and distinct contact with a cushion by the object ball. Incidental contact with a cushion as the object ball approaches the *called pocket* shall not be considered an "extra" cushion(s) that would otherwise disqualify a legal shot. Rebounding of the object ball in the *jaws* of the pocket before dropping shall not be considered "extra" cushions unless otherwise designated by the player.

6. It is a loss of game if a player commits three *successive fouls*.

ILLEGALLY POCKETED BALLS: All spotted; no penalty. **Special spotting rule:** When in the course of a legal scoring stroke, an additional ball(s) is pocketed, spotting of the ball(s) is delayed until the shooter's inning ends. Should a player score the last ball on the table while any illegally pocketed balls are being held for delayed spotting, those balls are then spotted so the player may continue his inning.

OBJECT BALLS JUMPED OFF THE TABLE: All spotted. The stroke is a foul, and the penalty for fouls is followed. The incoming player accepts the cue ball in position.

CUE BALL AFTER JUMPING THE TABLE OR SCRATCH: Incoming player has cue ball in hand behind the head string.

PENALTY FOR FOULS: The player committing the foul must spot one of his previously scored object balls for each foul committed. If a player fouls when he has no previously pocketed balls to spot up, he "owes" for such fouls, and must spot balls after each scoring inning until his "owed" fouls are eliminated. After fouls other than jumped cue ball or cue ball scratch, incoming player accepts the cue ball in position.

ONE POCKET

Except when clearly contradicted by these additional rules,
the **General Rules of Pocket Billiards** apply.

TYPE OF GAME: One Pocket is a unique game in which only two of the six pockets are employed for legal scoring. Any ball may be played and need not be called. What is required is that an object ball falls in the player's "target" pocket. It requires a wide variety of strokes, cue ball control, shot-making ability, patience and defensive strategy.

PLAYERS: 2, or 2 teams.

BALLS USED: Standard set of object balls 1-15, plus *cue ball*.

THE RACK: Standard *triangle* rack; balls placed entirely at random.

OBJECT OF THE GAME: To *score* a total of eight object balls in a player's target pocket before opponent.

SELECTION OF POCKETS: Prior to the opening break shot, starting player chooses one of the corner pockets on the foot end of the table as his target pocket; opponent then has the other foot end corner as his target pocket.

SCORING: A legally pocketed ball is scored as one ball for shooter. Any ball pocketed in opponent's target pocket counts, unless the cue ball should scratch on the same shot. If the shot constitutes a foul other than a scratch, the opponent is allowed to keep the ball. Shooter's inning ends on a scratch or foul and any balls pocketed in shooter's pocket do not count on a foul or scratch. In addition, the shooter is penalized one ball for a foul or scratch.

OPENING BREAK: Starting player must (1) legally pocket an object ball into his targeted pocket, or (2) cause the cue ball to contact an object ball and after contact, at least one object ball must contact a cushion. Failure to do so is a foul. NOTE: Cue ball does not have to strike a rail on the opening break.

RULES OF PLAY:

1. A legal shot requires that the cue ball contact an object ball and then (1) pocket an object ball, or (2) cause the cue ball or an object ball to contact a cushion. Failure to do so is a foul.

2. A legally pocketed ball in a target pocket entitles the shooter to remain at the table until he fails to pocket a ball in his target pocket on a legal shot. Player may shoot any object ball he chooses, and any ball pocketed in his target pocket on an otherwise legal stroke is a scored ball.

3. Balls pocketed in the four non-target pockets are "Illegally Pocketed Balls."

4. Balls pocketed by shooter in his opponent's target pocket are scored for the opponent, even if the stroke was a foul, but would not count if the cue ball should scratch or jump the table. However, if the stroke is not a foul and the shooter pockets a ball(s) in both target pockets, shooter's inning continues, with all legally pocketed balls scored to the appropriate player. If a shooter pockets a ball that brings the opponent's score to the number opponent needed to win the game, the shooter has lost.

5. When a player has the *cue ball in hand behind the head string* (as after a scratch) and all object balls are also behind the head string, the object ball nearest the head string may be *spotted* at his request. If two or more balls are an equal distance from the head string, the highest-numbered ball is spotted.

6. Three *successive fouls* by the same player is loss of game.

ILLEGALLY POCKETED BALLS: All spotted. **Special spotting rules:** When a ball(s) is pocketed in a non-target pocket, spotting is delayed until the shooter's inning ends. Should a player legally score the last ball(s) on the table while any illegally pocketed balls are being held for delayed spotting, those balls are then spotted so the player may continue his inning.

OBJECT BALLS JUMPED OFF THE TABLE: All spotted. The stroke is a foul, and penalty for fouls is followed. The incoming player accepts the cue ball in position.

CUE BALL AFTER JUMPING OFF THE TABLE OR SCRATCH: Incoming player has cue ball in hand behind the head string.

PENALTY FOR FOULS: The player committing the foul must spot one of his previously scored object balls for each foul committed. If a player who fouls has no previously pocketed balls to spot up, he "owes" for such fouls, and must spot balls after each scoring inning until his "owed" fouls are eliminated. After fouls other than jumped cue ball or cue ball scratch, incoming player accepts the cue ball in position.

THREE FOUL PENALTY: If a player scratches or fouls three consecutive turns at the table, it is a loss of game.

BREAKING SUBSEQUENT RACKS: If a "race" or set of games is being played as a match, players alternate the break shot in subsequent games.

OTHER POPULAR POCKET BILLIARDS GAMES

— BASEBALL POCKET BILLIARDS —

This game is played with twenty-one object balls, numbered from 1 to 21, and a white cue ball. The object balls are racked at the foot spot (in a 21-ball triangle). The 1-ball is placed on the foot spot, which is called "home plate." The 2- and 3-balls, respectively, are placed at the left and right corners of the triangle. The 9-ball, called the "pitcher," is placed near the center of the rack. (See Diagram 7.) Starting player has cue ball in hand.

SCORING: Players are credited with all balls legally pocketed. Each player has nine shots or innings at the table, which he plays in succession. In other words, each player continues at the table until he has had nine innings. An inning continues until a player misses or loses his turn as the result of a foul.

The number of runs scored correspond to the number on the balls pocketed by the player. If a player scores the 12- and 13-balls in one inning, he gets credit for twenty-five runs in that inning. Score is posted by innings on score sheet. The game ends when all players have completed nine innings of play.

The winner is the player with the most runs after all have played.

START OF PLAY: Rotation of play may be determined by lag or lot. Starting player has cue ball in hand within the string. The starting player is credited with all balls scored on the break shot. After the break, he continues, but must "call his shots"— ball and pocket.

SUBSEQUENT PLAY: Incoming players have balls racked and proceed as above, playing nine innings.

SPOTTING BALLS: If a player pockets a ball and makes a scratch, the object ball must be spotted on the "home plate" (foot spot). If home plate is occupied, balls are spotted according to general rules for spotting balls in pocket billiards.

SCRATCHES: If the player scratches, it completes his inning and an "O" is placed in that inning on the score sheet. He then plays the next inning. If a scratch is made and no object ball is pocketed, it is still regarded as a scoreless inning. Scratches are penalized by forfeit of all balls pocketed on foul stroke, plus last called ball legally pocketed. If player has no balls to his credit, he spots next called ball scored.

CALL SHOTS: If a player makes a called ball as designated, all other balls pocketed on the same stroke accrue to his credit. If he fails to pocket the called ball, however, and other balls drop in pockets, the pocketed balls are spotted, it counts as a scoreless inning and player continues, unless miss occurred in ninth inning.

NINE INNINGS: Any number of players may play baseball pocket billiards, but before the game is complete, all players must have nine innings at the table, but if a player runs all the balls before he completes nine innings of play, the balls are re-racked and player continues until he completes nine innings, and his total score is posted.

GENERAL RULES: Unless conflicting with provisions for this game, the **General Rules of Pocket Billiards** apply to **Baseball Pocket Billiards**.

Baseball Pocket Billiards

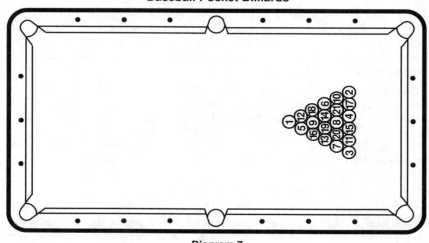

Diagram 7

—— BASIC POCKET BILLIARDS ——

Except when clearly contradicted by these additional rules,
the **General Rules of Pocket Billiards** apply.

TYPE OF GAME: The game of **Basic Pocket Billiards** is a combination of the call shot aspects of **14.1 Continuous** and the "anything goes" character of **Fifteen Ball**. It is a game well-suited for "mixed" (beginners and accomplished players) play, particularly in a team mode.

PLAYERS: 2, or 2 teams.

BALLS USED: Standard set of object balls 1-15, plus *cue ball*.

THE RACK: Standard *triangle* rack; balls placed entirely at random.

OBJECT OF THE GAME: To score eight balls before opponent.

SCORING: Any legally pocketed ball is scored as one ball.

OPENING BREAK: Starting player must (1) legally pocket an object ball into his targeted pocket, or (2) cause the cue ball to contact an object ball and after contact, at least one object ball must contact a cushion. Failure to do so is a foul. NOTE: Cue ball does not have to strike a rail on the opening break.

Failure is a *breaking violation*; opponent can accept the *table in position* and shoot, or require that the balls be reracked and offending player repeat the *opening break* until the requirements are satisfied.

If starting player pockets a ball on the opening break, it is a legally pocketed ball if no *foul* or other violation is committed, and he continues at the table. On all subsequent shots, however, he must comply with all the "Rules of Play" below.

RULES OF PLAY:

1. A legally pocketed ball entitles shooter to continue at the table until he fails to pocket a ball on a legal shot. Player may shoot any ball he chooses, but before he shoots must designate a single ball that he will pocket; he need **not** indicate into which pocket the ball will score, *kisses, caroms, combinations* or cushions (all of which are legal).

2. On all shots subsequent to the opening break, player must cause the cue ball to contact an object ball, and then (1) pocket an object ball, or (2) cause an object ball or the cue ball to contact a cushion. Failure to do so is a foul.

3. When a player has the cue ball in hand behind the head string and all remaining object balls are behind the head string as well, the object ball nearest the head string may be spotted on the foot spot at his request. If two or more balls are an equal distance from the head string, the player may designate which of the equidistant balls he desires to be spotted.

ILLEGALLY POCKETED BALLS: All *spotted*, no penalty.

OBJECT BALLS JUMPED OFF THE TABLE: All spotted. The stroke is a foul, and the penalty for fouls is followed.

CUE BALL AFTER JUMPING OFF THE TABLE OR SCRATCH: All spotted. The stroke is a foul, and the penalty for fouls is followed.

PENALTY FOR FOULS: One scored ball is returned to the table (spotted) by fouling player for each foul committed. If player who fouls has no previously pocketed balls to spot up, he "owes" for such fouls, and must spot balls after each scoring inning until his "owed" fouls are eliminated. After fouls other than cue ball jump or cue ball *scratch*, incoming player accepts cue ball in position.

BOTTLE POOL

Except when clearly contradicted by these additional rules,
the **General Rules of Pocket Billiards** apply.

TYPE OF GAME: A unique pocket billiard game, **Bottle Pool** requires the use of an inexpensive but specially shaped and balanced leather or plastic container ("bottle" or "*shaker bottle*"), shaped much like some disposable beverage bottles. The play of Bottle Pool combines the ball pocketing abilities of pocket billiards with the carom-making requirements of *carom* games.

PLAYERS: 2 or more.

BALLS USED: Object balls 1 and 2, plus *cue ball*.

THE RACK: No triangle needed; at the start of the game, the 1-ball is frozen to the *foot cushion,* centered on the first diamond in from the racker's right corner pocket; the 2-ball is *frozen* to the *foot cushion*, centered on the first diamond in from the racker's left corner pocket; the bottle is placed open end down on the *center spot.* (See Diagram 8.)

OBJECT OF THE GAME: To score exactly 31 points prior to opponent(s).

SCORING: There are five scoring possibilities. A player executing a legal stroke scores as follows:

(1) Pocketing the 1-ball: one point.

(2) Pocketing the 2-ball: two points.

(3) *Carom* of the cue ball on the two object balls: one point.

(4) Carom of the cue ball from an object ball(s) to the bottle which knocks the bottle onto its side: five points.

(5) Carom of the cue ball from an object ball(s) to the bottle which stands the bottle onto its base: automatic win of the game.

Should a player accomplish more than one scoring possibility on a shot, he scores for each; a single shot can result in a total of nine points scored.

Since **exactly** 31 points must be scored for victory (unless #5 above applies), a player must not exceed 31; if he does, his inning ends and his score becomes only the total by which he exceeded 31.

OPENING BREAK: No "break shot" as such. Beginning with *cue ball in hand behind the head string,* starting player must cause the cue ball to contact either the 1-ball or the 2-ball. If he fails to do so, incoming player can require that offending player repeat the opening shot until that requirement is satisfied.

RULES OF PLAY:

1. A legally executed scoring stroke entitles shooter to continue at the table until he fails to legally score on a shot, exceeds 31 points on a shot, causes an

object ball to contact the bottle before the cue ball contacts the bottle (the entire shot is invalid and *inning* ends), or causes the bottle to be forced off the table or into a pocket (the entire shot is invalid and inning ends).

Bottle Pool

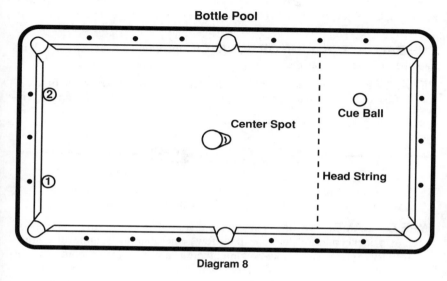

Diagram 8

2. On all shots, player must cause the cue ball to contact an object ball. Failure to do so is a foul.

3. Cue ball must contact an object ball before it contacts the bottle. Failure to do so is a foul.

4. If player causes the bottle to be upset, or upended by an object ball, the shot is a foul.

5. Player loses the game if he fouls in each of three consecutive innings at the table.

REPLACING UPSET BOTTLE: Whenever the bottle is upset, it is replaced on the table, open end down, with the open end as close as possible to its position when the bottle came to rest. It is, of course, replaced prior to the next shot.

When the bottle is forced off the table or into a pocket (or into such position that the open end is over the pocket opening making replacement as in the preceding paragraph impossible), the bottle is replaced on the center spot. If occupied, the head spot; if occupied, the foot spot; if occupied, hold out until center spot is vacant.

ILLEGALLY POCKETED BALLS: All spotted. The stroke is a foul, and the penalty for fouls is followed.

OBJECT BALLS JUMPED OFF THE TABLE: All spotted. The stroke is a foul, and the penalty for fouls is followed.

SPECIAL SPOTTING RULES: After each shot is completed, any pocketed object balls are spotted prior to the next shot. They are spotted in the positions as at the start of the game. If a ball or the bottle prevents the free placement of an object ball to be spotted, the object ball is spotted on the center spot; if that is also occupied, the object ball is then spotted on the head spot. If both object balls are being spotted, follow the above, first spotting the 1-ball, then the 2-ball.

CUE BALL AFTER JUMP OR SCRATCH: Incoming player has cue ball in hand behind the head string.

PENALTY FOR FOULS: One point is deducted from offender's score for each foul. After fouls other than cue ball jump or cue ball *scratch,* incoming player

——— BOWLLIARDS ———

Except when clearly contradicted by these additional rules,
the **General Rules of Pocket Billiards** apply.

TYPE OF GAME: Bowlliards is a game that applies the scoring concepts of bowling to pocket billiards. It is one of the few games that can be quite interesting as a solitary exercise since, like bowling, there is a perfect game score to strive for, and a player can measure his improvement quite easily over the course of time playing Bowlliards.

PLAYERS: Any number.

BALLS USED: Any ten objects balls, plus *cue ball.*

THE RACK: Standard triangle position (front apex ball on *foot spot*), using a 1-2-3-4 rack configuration.

OBJECT OF THE GAME: To score a perfect score of 300 points in 10 frames (innings) in solitary play. In competition, to score a higher point total in 10 innings than opponent(s).

SCORING: Each legally pocketed ball is scored as one point, regardless of ball number. The points scored as per the "Rules of Play" below are treated exactly as is the pinfall in bowling.

OPENING BREAK: At the start of player's inning (frame), he has a *free break* (no special balls-to-cushion or other requirements once break stroke commences, and a jumped or *scratched* cue ball is without penalty). Any balls pocketed on the break are *spotted,* and player then follows his break by beginning scoring play with object balls in position and *cue ball in hand behind the head string.* (The opening break takes place at the start of every inning.)

RULES OF PLAY:
   1. A legally pocketed ball entitles shooter to continue at the table until he fails to pocket a *called ball* on a shot, or until he has scored the maximum total per

inning possible (10). Player may shoot any ball he chooses, but before he shoots, must designate a single ball that he will pocket and the pocket into which the ball will score; he need not indicate *kisses, caroms, combinations* or *cushions* (none of which are illegal).

2. Player has two chances to pocket the 10 possible balls of each frame. If player legally pockets ten consecutive balls on his first chance of a frame, that frame is completed and player scores the frame exactly as a strike in bowling. If player fails to pocket ten consecutive balls on his first chance, he takes his second chance immediately. If he succeeds in legally pocketing the remaining balls of the ten on his second chance, the frame is completed and player scores it exactly as a spare in bowling. If player fails to legally pocket all ten balls in two chances, the frame is then completed and is scored just as in bowling; a "strike" in the tenth inning earns two extra shots, a spare one extra shot.

3. If players tie for high game total in competition, additional extra innings are played alternately by the tied players, with the first player posting a superior score to that of his opponent(s) being the winner ("sudden death").

ILLEGALLY POCKETED BALLS: On the break, illegally pocketed balls are spotted prior to player beginning his scoring play (first chance of the frame). During scoring play, illegally pocketed balls are spotted.

OBJECT BALLS JUMPED OFF THE TABLE: All spotted. The stroke is a foul, and the penalty for fouls is followed.

CUE BALL AFTER JUMP OR SCRATCH: Only applies if occuring as player's first foul of a frame, player has cue ball in hand behind the head string to begin his second chance of the frame.

PENALTY FOR FOULS: One point is deducted from offender's score for each *foul*. If foul ends player's first chance of a frame, he has cue ball in hand behind the head string to begin his second chance of the frame.

——————— BUMPER POOL ———————

Rules and Regulations (Reprinted with permission of
The Valley Company, Bay City, Michigan)

1. Bumper Pool® is played by two players or by four as partners.

2. Each side has five red balls or five white balls, one of each color being a marked cue ball.

3. To set up Bumper Pool, place two red balls on each side of the white cup (pocket) on markers, placing marked red ball directly in front of white cup. Place white balls in same position around the red cup (pocket).

4. Both players shoot marked ball at the same time, hitting first the side-cushion, banking the ball into or near his color cup. The player who plays his ball

into or nearest his cup shoots again. Marked cue balls must be pocketed first. If a player sinks another ball before his marked ball is pocketed, his opponent may remove two of his own balls and drop them into his cup. In the event that both marked balls are pocketed on first shots each player takes one of remaining balls and spots it in front of cup and both shoot at same time, just as they did with marked balls. From there on they take turns beginning with the player who pockets his ball or is nearest to his cup.

Bumper Pool

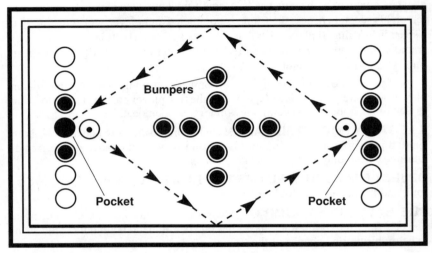

Diagram 9

5. A player receives another shot upon sinking his own color ball in his own color cup.

6. In the event that a player causes a ball to leave the table, his opponent may place this ball anywhere he wishes, and in addition can remove two of his own balls and drop them into his cup as an additional bonus.

7. If a player sinks one of his opponent's balls there is no penalty, but if he sinks one of his own balls into his opponent's cup, or shoots one of his opponent's balls, his opponent may then drop two of his own balls into his cup.

8. No player is allowed to jump his ball over balls or bumpers in making shots. Penalty for this will be the same as in Rule 7.

9. The first player or team to sink all five balls is the winner, except that player forfeits game if he shoots his last ball into his opponent's cup.

10. The length of time that the winners may continue playing is governed by House Rule.

COWBOY

Except when clearly contradicted by these additional rules,
the **General Rules of Pocket Billiards** apply.

TYPE OF GAME: Cowboy is another game that combines carom and pocket
billiards skills, and employs a very unusual set of rules. Certainly a change of pace
game; how many games have you played in which the cue ball **must** be pocketed
on a carom of the 1-ball on the last shot??!

PLAYERS: Any number.

BALLS USED: Object balls 1, 3 and 5, plus the *cue ball.*

THE RACK: No *triangle* needed; the 1-ball is placed on the *head spot,* the 3-ball
on the *foot spot,* and the 5-ball on the *center spot.*

OBJECT OF THE GAME: To score 101 points prior to opponent(s).

Cowboy Pocket Billiards

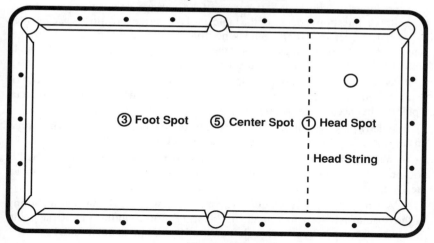

Diagram 10

SCORING: The first ninety points exactly may be scored by any of these means
on legal scoring strokes:

(1) pocketing any of the objects balls: points equal to the balls' numbers; or

(2) *carom* of the cue ball off two of the object balls: one point; or

(3) carom of the cue ball off the three object balls: two points.

Points 91 through 100 (exactly) must, and may only, be scored by execution
of carom shots 2 and 3 above.

Point 101 (winning point) must be scored by caroming the cue ball off the 1-ball into a *called pocket* without the cue ball contacting any other object ball.

Should a player accomplish more than one scoring possibility permitted by these rules, he scores for each; thus a single shot can result in a total of 11 points scored.

OPENING BREAK: No "break shot" as such. Beginning with *cue ball in hand behind the head string,* starting player must cause the cue ball to contact the 3-ball first. If starting player fails to do so, incoming player has choice of (1) requiring starting player to repeat the opening shot, or (2) executing the opening shot himself.

RULES OF PLAY:

1. A legally executed shot, conforming to the requirements of "Scoring," entitles shooter to continue at the table until he fails to legally execute and score on a shot.

2. On all shots, player must cause the cue ball to contact an object ball, and then the cue ball or object ball must contact a *cushion.* Failure to do so is a foul.

3. At the completion of each shot, any pocketed object balls are *spotted* on their same positions as at the start of the game. If the appropriate position is occupied, the ball(s) in question remain off the table until the correct position is vacant after a shot. If, however, the 1-ball would be held out as a player with exactly 100 points is to shoot, the balls are all placed as at the start of the game, and the player shoots with cue ball in hand behind the head string.

4. When a player scores his 90th point, the shot must score the number of points exactly needed to reach 90; if the shot producing the 90th point also scores a point(s) in excess of 90 for the player, the shot is a *foul.*

5. When a player is playing for points 91 through 100 (which must all be scored on *caroms* solely), it is a foul to pocket an object ball on a shot.

6. When a player is playing for his 101st point, it is a foul if the cue ball is pocketed in a pocket other than the one called, of if the cue balls fails to contact the 1-ball, or if the cue ball contacts any other object ball.

7. When a player pockets the cue ball on an otherwise legal shot, and according to the special requirements given in "Scoring" for counting the 101st point, pocketing the cue ball on such a shot on the 101st point is not a foul.

8. Player loses the game if he fouls in each of three consecutive plays at the table.

ILLEGALLY POCKETED BALLS: All spotted per the provision of Rule of Play 3 (above), with no penalty, **except** in the special cases covered by the Rules of Play 4 and 5.

OBJECT BALLS JUMPED OFF THE TABLE: All spotted. The stroke is a foul, and the penalty for fouls is followed.

CUE BALL AFTER JUMP OR SCRATCH: Incoming player has cue ball in hand behind the head string.

PENALTY FOR FOULS: No point deduction, but any points scored on previous shots of the inning are not scored, and player's inning ends. After fouls other than cue ball jump or cue ball *scratch,* incoming player accepts the cue ball in position.

——————— CRIBBAGE ———————

Except when clearly contradicted by these additional rules,
the **General Rules of Pocket Billiards** apply.

TYPE OF GAME: Cribbage Pocket Billiards derives its name from the fact that a score can be made (with two exceptions) only by pocketing two consecutive balls which add up to fifteen; a similarity exists with the popular card game of Cribbage. In a sense, it represents a combination of a call-shot game and a set-order game, and is a bit different and quite interesting to play.

PLAYERS: 2.

BALLS USED: Standard set of object balls 1-15 plus *cue ball.*

THE RACK: Standard *triangle* rack, with the 15-ball in the center; with the exception that no two of the three corner balls shall add up to a total of fifteen points, all other balls may be placed entirely at random.

OBJECT OF THE GAME: To *score* five points (cribbages) out of a possible total of eight.

DEFINITION OF A CRIBBAGE: A cribbage is a pair of object balls, legally pocketed, numerically totaling 15. There are just these seven regular cribbages: 1-14, 2-13, 3-12, 4-11, 5-10, 6-9 and 7-8. No other ball combinations can be cribbages except that when all seven regular cribbages have been legally pocketed, the 15 ball becomes a legal cribbage by itself.

SCORING: Each legally pocketed cribbage counts one point for scoring player.

OPENING BREAK: Starting player must attempt an *open break.* Failure to do so is a *breaking violation*; opponent has the choice of (1) requiring offending player to repeat the opening break (until requirements are satisfied), or (2) playing the opening break shot himself.

Starting player is not required to call his shot; if any balls are pocketed on the break shot, they accrue to him and he may continue at the table.

RULES OF PLAY:

1. To legally pocket a cribbage, the two balls must be pocketed in the same inning. When a player has legally pocketed a single ball on a shot, he must legally pocket the appropriate companion ball on his next shot, or it is a *foul.*

2. If a player scores a legal cribbage, he can continue his inning and attempt to score more cribbages in the same inning.

3. When not "on a cribbage," if a player pockets two or more balls on a shot that do not constitute a cribbage, he may next pocket any of the proper companion balls as he chooses, but must successively pocket each of those companion balls if he is to continue at the table. If he fails, it is a foul. If, while satisfying the requirements of scoring companion balls, other ball(s) are incidentally pocketed, they likewise accrue to him; he must continue to complete one of the cribbages he is "on" on each successive stroke (though in no special order). Failure to do so is a foul; all balls of uncompleted cribbages are spotted.

4. When a ball is pocketed legally, but player fails to complete the cribbage legally during the same inning, the ball is spotted.

5. On all shots, player must cause the cue ball to contact an object ball and then either (1) pocket an object ball, or (2) cause an object ball or the cue ball to contact a cushion. Failure to do so is a foul.

6. Player loses the game if he commits three *successive fouls*.

7. If the 15-ball is pocketed before all the other cribbages have been legally pocketed, it is an illegally pocketed ball and is *spotted* immediately following the stroke (not inning) on which it was pocketed. No penalty.

8. When a player has the *cue ball in hand behind the head string* (as after a scratch) and all the object balls are also behind the head string, the object ball nearest the head string may be spotted on the foot spot at his request. If two or more balls are an equal distance from the head string, the player may also designate which of the equidistant balls he desires to be spotted.

ILLEGALLY POCKETED BALLS: All spotted; no penalty.

OBJECT BALLS JUMPED OFF THE TABLE: All spotted. The stroke is a foul, and the penalty for fouls is followed.

CUE BALL AFTER JUMPING OFF THE TABLE OR SCRATCH: Incoming player has cue ball in hand behind the head string.

PENALTY FOR FOULS: Inning ends; no point or ball penalty (except per Rule of Play 6 above). Incoming player has the option of (1) accepting the table in position and shooting, or (2) shooting with cue ball in hand behind the head string.

CUT-THROAT

Except when clearly contradicted by these additional rules,
the **General Rules of Pocket Billiards** apply.

TYPE OF GAME: Cut-Throat (also known as Elimination) is a very popular game in social situations, rather than for serious competitive play. It is very enjoyable to play—fast and with simple rules. A perfect game when an odd number of participants are available.

PLAYERS: 3 or 5.

BALLS USED: Standard set of object balls 1-15 plus *cue ball*.

THE RACK: Standard *triangle* rack with the 1 ball on the foot spot, and the 6 and 11 balls on the two corners; all other balls placed at random.

DETERMINATION OF GROUPS: In three-player game, starting player has the group of balls 1-5; second player has balls 6-10; third player has balls 11-15. In five-player game, starting player 1-3; second player 4-6; third 7-9; fourth 10-12; and fifth 13-15.

OBJECT OF THE GAME: To legally pocket your opponents' balls before the opponents legally pocket your group of balls.

SCORING: Group balls have no point value. The player with a ball(s) still on the table, when all the other groups' balls are legally pocketed, wins the game.

OPENING BREAK: Starting player must make an *open break*. If he fails to do so, incoming player may (1) accept the *table in position* and shoot, or (2) require that the balls be reracked and shoot the opening break himself. All balls pocketed on a legal break remain pocketed.

RULES OF PLAY:

1. Players must decide prior to the game whether they are playing call shot or not.

2. A legal shot requires that the cue ball's first contact be with an opponents' object ball. On all shots, player must cause the cue ball to contact an object ball and then either (1) pocket an object ball, or (2) cause any object ball or the cue ball to contact a cushion. Failure to meet these requirements is a foul. Any legally pocketed ball entitles shooter to continue at the table until he fails to pocket an object ball on a shot. (Also see exception: Rule of Play 4.)

3. If player pockets any opponents' balls on an illegal shot, they are spotted; but if he pockets his own group balls on an illegal shot, they remain pocketed. If player pockets the last ball of his own group, whether or not on a legal shot, it remains pocketed and his inning ends.

4. When a player's last group ball is legally pocketed, he is eliminated from the shooting rotation. He remains eliminated for the duration of the game **unless** a foul is committed by a player still in the game; when a player is reinstated due to a foul, he resumes his normal position in the original order of play.

5. When a player has the *cue ball in hand behind the head string* (as after a scratch), and all balls of all opponents' groups are behind the head string, the object ball nearest the head string may, at the shooter's request, be spotted on the foot spot. If two or more balls are an equal distance from the head string, the player may designate which of the equidistant balls he desires to be spotted.

6. When successive games are being played, the order of play for the next

game is the same as the order of final elimination in the preceding game. (First player eliminated breaks; winner shoots last; others in order of elimination.)

ILLEGALLY POCKETED BALLS: Opponents' group balls are *spotted;* no penalty. Shooter's group balls remain pocketed, no penalty.

OBJECT BALLS JUMPED OFF THE TABLE: All spotted. The stroke is a foul, and the penalty for fouls is followed. The incoming player accepts the cue ball in position.

CUE BALL AFTER JUMPING OFF THE TABLE OR SCRATCH: Incoming player has cue ball in hand behind the head string.

PENALTY FOR FOULS: Shooter's inning ends. In addition, one ball from each of the opponents' groups that is off the table is brought back into play. Players who had been eliminated can be reinstated at any time until the game is over. If a player's group has no pocketed balls at the time of a foul by one of his opponents, then the penalty has no effect on that group or player; the penalty is not carried forward.

─────── EQUAL OFFENSE ───────

Except when clearly contradicted by these additional rules,
the **General Rules of Pocket Billiards** apply.

TYPE OF GAME: Equal Offense is a game in which each player shoots until he misses a shot, fouls or pockets the maximum amount of balls allowed for the inning. The winner is determined by the total inning score (similar to bowling). Based on **14.1 Continuous**, the game is ideal for leagues, tournaments, handicapping and averaging; fair, fun and interesting for beginners as well as the advanced player. Although copyrighted by Jerry Briesath, he has placed no restrictions on its use.

PLAYERS: Any number.

BALLS USED: Standard set of objects balls 1-15, plus *cue ball.*

THE RACK: Standard *triangle* rack; balls placed entirely at random. The balls are racked at the beginning of each inning for each player.

OBJECT OF THE GAME: To *score* more total points than opponent(s) in a predetermined number of innings (200 points in 10 innings maximum).

SCORING: Any legally pocketed ball counts one point for shooter.

OPENING BREAK: At the start of each player's inning, he has a *free break* (no special balls to cushion or other requirements once break stroke commences, and a jumped or *scratched* cue ball is without penalty). Any balls pocketed on the break are spotted, and player then begins shooting with object balls in position and *cue ball in hand behind the head string*. The *opening break* takes place at the start of every inning of each player (10 times per match in Championship play for each player).

RULES OF PLAY:

1. Player may shoot any ball he chooses, but before he shoots must designate an object ball and a *called pocket*. He need not indicate *kisses, caroms, combinations* or *cushions* (none of which are illegal). A legally pocketed ball entitles the shooter to continue at the table until he fails to pocket a *called ball*, or until he has scored the maximum total per inning permissible (20 points in championship play).

2. Player is entitled to any additional balls pocketed on a shot, as long as he pockets his called ball.

3. Shooting order for subsequent innings is determined by the scoring results of preceding innings – player with the highest score shooting first. In the event of a tie inning, the order does not change.

4. If players are tied for high match total (10 inning) score, additional innings are played by each tied player with the first player posting a superior score to his opponent(s) in an equal number of innings being the winner ("sudden death").

OBJECT BALLS JUMPED OFF THE TABLE: The stroke is a foul, and the penalty for fouls is followed.

CUE BALL AFTER JUMP OFF THE TABLE OR SCRATCH: Does not apply to Equal Offense, since a jumped or scratched cue ball ends player's inning, and all players' innings begin with the opening break.

PENALTY FOR FOULS: No point penalty; player's inning ends.

SOME VARIATIONS: For purposes of scheduling, handicapping, etc., variations can be made as follows:

1. A given number of misses or *fouls* may be allowed per inning (use **14.1 Continuous** rules for "Cue Ball After Jump or Scratch").

2. Maximum number of balls per inning permissible may be increased or decreased.

3. Number of innings constituting a *match* may be increased or decreased.

4. Each player's inning may be restricted by a time limit.

5. Combinations of any of the variations above may be utilized, and may be applied in a non-uniform manner as a means of handicapping players.

6. As an exercise for beginners to progress in finding patterns of play, three chances should be allowed (two misses, *cue ball in hand*) to reach a score of 15. An intermediate player should be allowed two chances. The ten inning perfect score would thus be 150.

7. Third miss ends player's inning.

FIFTEEN BALL

Except when clearly contradicted by these additional rules,
the **General Rules of Pocket Billiards** apply.

TYPE OF GAME: Fifteen Ball is a basic game variation that does not require calling balls or pockets, and yet rewards good shot selection because scoring is based on the numerical values of the balls (numbers) as in **Rotation.** It is a game well-suited for developing skills at beginning and intermediate player levels.

PLAYERS: 2 or more, though 2 players are generally preferred.

BALLS USED: Standard set of object balls 1-15, plus *cue ball.*

THE RACK: Standard *triangle* rack with the 15-ball on the *foot spot;* other balls have no exact positions, but the higher numbered balls are placed at the front of the rack near the 15-ball, with the lower numbered balls near the back of the rack.

OBJECT OF THE GAME: To score balls of greater total point value than opponent(s).

SCORING: Each legally pocketed object ball has a point value equal to its number. Game ends when a player's point total mathematically eliminates opponent(s) [61 in a two player game]. If two or more players tie for highest point total, the tied player legally pocketing the last object ball is credited with the game.

OPENING BREAK: Starting player must either (1) pocket a ball (does **not** have to call either ball or pocket), or (2) cause the cue ball to contact an object ball, and then the cue ball and two object balls must contact a *cushion.* If he fails to do so, incoming player has choice of (1) accepting the *table in position* and shooting, or (2) having the balls reracked and shooting the opening break himself, or (3) requiring offending player to repeat the opening break.

RULES OF PLAY:

1. Any ball pocketed on a legal shot entitles shooter to continue at the table until he fails to do so.

2. On all shots subsequent to the opening break, player must cause the cue ball to contact an object ball, and then either (1) pocket an object ball, or (2) cause an object ball or the cue ball to contact a cushion. Failure to do so is a foul.

3. When a player has the *cue ball in hand behind the head string* (as after a scratch) and all object balls are also behind the head string, the object ball nearest the head string may be spotted on the foot spot at his request. If two or more balls are an equal distance from the head string, the player may designate which of the equidistant balls he desires to be spotted.

ILLEGALLY POCKETED BALLS: All spotted; no penalty.

OBJECT BALLS JUMPED OFF THE TABLE: All spotted. The stroke is a foul, and the penalty for fouls is followed.

CUE BALL AFTER JUMPING OFF TABLE OR SCRATCH: Incoming player has cue ball in hand behind the head string.

PENALTY FOR FOULS: Three points are deducted from the offender's score for each foul committed. After fouls other than jumped cue ball or cue ball *scratch,* incoming player accepts the table in position.

FORTY-ONE

Except when clearly contradicted by these additional rules,
the **General Rules of Pocket Billiards** apply.

TYPE OF GAME: Forty-One Pocket Billiards is another game that is well-suited bfor social play at parties or other gatherings where players of mixed abilities will take part. Since no one knows what number *"pea"* is held by his opponent(s), it is difficult to play defensively. In addition, the rules are designed to greatly equalize all the players' chances. An unusual and interesting game.

PLAYERS: 2 to 15 (though 3, 4, or 5 are generally preferred).

BALLS USED: Standard set of object balls 1-15 plus *cue ball.* A set of fifteen numbered peas (or *"pills"*) and a *shake bottle* are also used.

THE RACK: Standard *triangle* rack with balls placed entirely at random.

DETERMINING PRIVATE NUMBERS: After the balls are racked but before play begins, each player is given a pea from the shake bottle containing the peas numbered from 1-15. The number of the pea is the player's private number and is kept secret.

OBJECT OF THE GAME: To score points which, when added to the player's private number, total exactly forty-one.

SCORING: Each legally pocketed ball has a point value equal to its number.

OPENING BREAK: Starting player must make an *open break.* He is not obligated to pocket a ball on the break shot; but if he fails to make a legal *open break,* it is a foul.

RULES OF PLAY:

1. Any ball(s) scored on a legal stroke count for the shooter. Players may shoot any ball and need not call ball, pocket or mode of shot.

2. A player is permitted only one shot or turn per inning, regardless of whether or not he scores.

3. An illegally pocketed ball is a foul, and does not score for the shooter.

4. On all shots, player must cause the cue ball to contact an object ball and then either (1) pocket an object ball, or (2) cause an object ball or the cue ball to contact a cushion. Failure to do so is a foul.

5. When a player has the *cue ball in hand behind the head string* (as after a scratch) and all object balls are also behind the head string, the object ball nearest the head string may be spotted on the foot spot at his request. If two or more balls are an equal distance from the head string, the player may designate which of the equidistant balls he desires to be spotted.

6. When player has a total count of forty-one, he must announce his victory and present his pea for confirmation before the next player shoots. If he fails to declare his forty-one total until the next player has shot, he must wait until his next turn to so declare. If, in the meantime, another player succeeds in attaining a legal total count of forty-one and properly declares, the latter player wins the game.

7. If a player totals more than forty-one points, he has "burst" and must so declare immediately (before the next player shoots). All balls the burst player had pocketed are spotted, and the burst player may request a new pea prior to his next turn if he so desires. Any player who bursts and does not declare it prior to the following player's shot is disqualified from further play in the game; if a two-player game, his opponent is automatically the winner.

8. If all balls are pocketed prior to any player attaining a total count of forty-one, the player whose count is closest to forty-one wins the game. If two or more players are tied for nearest to forty-one in this situation, the game is a tie.

ILLEGALLY POCKETED BALLS: All spotted; no penalty.

OBJECT BALLS JUMPED OFF THE TABLE: All spotted. The stroke is a foul, and the penalty for fouls is followed.

CUE BALL AFTER JUMPING OFF THE TABLE OR SCRATCH: Incoming player has cue ball in hand behind the head string.

PENALTY FOR FOULS: The player committing a foul must spot one of his previously scored object balls for each foul committed. If a player has no previously pocketed balls to his credit when he commits a foul, he is exempt from a penalty for that particular foul.

HONOLULU

Except when clearly contradicted by these additional rules,
the **General Rules of Pocket Billiards** apply.

TYPE OF GAME: Honolulu is a unique and fascinating pocket billiard game that confronts the player with an unending kaleidoscope of strategic and shot-making challenges.

Essentially, Honolulu is just a game of one-rack call shot. Call any ball in any pocket; score one point per legally pocketed ball; the first player to make eight points wins. (Said score, incidentally, being kept the same as in One Pocket: Put your balls in your bin (just pick a side) and re-spot out of your bin any time you scratch or foul.)

The major critical difference being — absolutely no "straight-in" shots are allowed. Each and every legally pocketed ball must be made by means of either (1) a bank, (2) a combination, (3) a carom, (4) a "kick" shot, or (5) some combination thereof.

PLAYERS: 2, or 2 teams.

BALLS USED: Standard set of 15 object balls, plus cue ball.

THE RACK: Standard triangle; balls racked at random.

OBJECT OF GAME: Winner of game must score eight (8) points before opponent. (Each legally pocketed ball scores one (1) point.)

SCORING: Player must call ball and pocket. If called ball is made in designated pocket by means of either a bank, combination, carom, or kick shot (or any combination thereof), it is considered a legally pocketed ball and scores one (1) point.

It is not necessary to call or specify kisses, caroms, rails, etc.

Only called balls legally score. Any balls accidentally (or illegally) pocketed are re-spotted at end of inning. Note: 1985 Vaso Amendment may be implemented at player's option. To wit: Shooter may call any number of balls (two or more) on any one shot — as long as all balls called are pocketed as called — or none are scored. In other words, call all you want, but make all you call — or none qualify. Shooter calling two balls but pocketing only one a) loses inning and b) must re-spot pocketed ball.

KICK SHOTS: No short-rail kicks. Kick shots are legal only when cue ball is first banked off rail not connected with designated pocket (or if cue ball is banked off any two, or more, rails before striking object ball). (See Diagram 11.)

Honolulu Pocket Billiards

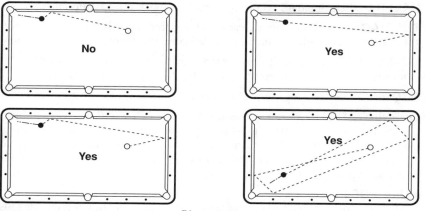

Diagram 11

OPENING BREAK: On the opening break the shooter must either (1) call and pocket a ball out of the rack, or (2) cause two object balls plus the cue ball to hit the cushion after striking rack with cue ball.

Failure to do either is a foul. Penalty: One (1) point. Incoming player accepts cue ball where it lies. Breaker owes one (1) ball (i.e., must re-spot first ball he legally pockets).

All subsequent play is subject to standard B.C.A Pocket Billiard Regulations. (Legal safety: Contact between cue ball and object ball, after which either cue ball — or object ball — or both — hit a cushion.)

FOULS AND PENALTIES: One (1) point penalty (one ball either re-spotted or owed) per scratch or foul. Following scratch, incoming player has cue ball in hand in kitchen; following foul, incoming shooter accepts cue ball where it lies.

The accidental touching or moving of any ball on the table is considered a foul.

In Honolulu there is no three consecutive foul penalty.

ILLEGALLY POCKETED BALLS: Are all re-spotted at end of inning.

LINE-UP

Except when clearly contradicted by these additional rules,
the **General Rules of Pocket Billiards** apply.

TYPE OF GAME: Line-Up is a forerunner of **14.1 Continuous.** This is how they did it way back then!

PLAYERS: 2.

BALLS USED: Standard set of object balls numbered 1-15, plus *cue ball.*

THE RACK: Standard *triangle* rack with the front apex ball on the *foot spot,* 1-ball on the rack's right corner, 5-ball on left corner; other balls placed at random.

OBJECT OF THE GAME: To score the predetermined point total (usually 150 in tournaments, or any agreed upon total) for game prior to opponent.

SCORING: Any ball legally pocketed counts one point for shooter.

OPENING BREAK: Starting player must pocket a *called ball* or drive two object balls to a *cushion*. If he fails to do so, he is assessed a two point penalty. Incoming player may accept the *table in position* and shoot, or require that offender repeat the opening break until the requirements are satisfied. Each successive failure is a two point penalty for offending player.

RULES OF PLAY:

1. A legally pocketed ball entitles shooter to continue at the table until he fails to pocket a called ball on a shot. Player may shoot any ball he chooses, but before

he shoots, must designate the ball he will pocket and the pocket into which the ball will score; he need indicate no other detail.

2. On all shots, player must cause the cue ball to contact an object ball and then either (1) pocket an object ball, or (2) cause the cue ball or any object ball to contact a cushion. Failure to do so is a *foul*.

3. A player may call a *safety* rather than an object ball if he so desires (for defensive purposes). Safety play is legal, but must comply with all applicable rules. Player's inning ends when safety is played, and pocketed balls are not scored. Any object ball pocketed on a called safety is *spotted*.

4. When the fifteenth ball of the rack has been pocketed, shooter records his scored balls from the rack. The balls are then spotted, and player continues shooting, playing the cue ball from where it came to rest after preceding shot, before the balls were spotted. (If player misses or fouls during the rack, he records his score and incoming player shoots, accepting the table in position.)

ILLEGALLY POCKETED BALLS: All spotted; no penalty.

OBJECT BALLS JUMPED OFF THE TABLE: All spotted. The stroke is a foul, and the penalty for fouls is followed.

CUE BALL AFTER JUMPING OFF THE TABLE OR SCRATCH: Incoming player has *cue ball in hand behind the head string* (unless the foul was a third successive foul; see "Successive Fouls Penalty").

PENALTY FOR FOULS: One point is deducted from offender's score for each foul committed, **unless** the foul is a third *successive foul* (see "Successive Fouls Penalty"). After fouls other than cue ball jump, cue ball *scratch,* or third *successive foul,* incoming player accepts the table in position.

SUCCESSIVE FOULS PENALTY: If a player commits three successive fouls, he is penalized one point for each foul, and an additional deduction of fifteen points. The balls are reracked and offending player is required to break the balls under the requirements of the opening break.

─────── MR. AND MRS. ───────

Except when clearly contradicted by these additional rules,
the **General Rules of Pocket Billiards** apply.

TYPE OF GAME: Mr. and Mrs. (also called Boy Meets Girl) is a game that combines the general forms of **Rotation** and **Basic Pocket Billiards**. The rules are different for players of widely differing skill levels.

PLAYERS: Any number from two to six.

BALLS USED: Standard set of object balls numbered 1-15, plus *cue ball.*

THE RACK: Standard *triangle* rack with the 1-ball on the *foot spot,* 2-ball on racker's right corner, 3-ball on left corner, 15-ball in the center. All other balls are placed at random.

OBJECT OF THE GAME: To score balls of greater total point value than opponent(s).

SCORING: Each legally pocketed object ball has a point value equal to its number. Game ends when a player's point total mathematically eliminates opponents(s) – 61 points in a 2-player game. If two or more players tie for highest point total, the tied player that legally pocketed the last object ball is credited with a game won.

OPENING BREAK: Starting player must cause the cue ball's first contact to be with the 1-ball. If starting player fails to meet this requirement, incoming player has the choice of (1) accepting the *table in position* and shooting, or (2) requiring that the balls be reracked and offending player repeat the *opening break.*

RULES OF PLAY:

1. A legally pocketed ball entitles shooter to continue at the table until he fails to legally pocket a ball.

2. On all shots, more skilled player must cause the cue ball's first contact with a ball to be with the lowest-numbered object ball on the table and then either (1) pocket a ball, or (2) cause the cue ball or any object ball to contact a *cushion.* Failure to do so is a foul.

3. Less skilled player may shoot any ball he chooses, regardless of number. He need not call ball, pocket or mode of shot. Any ball pocketed on a legal shot is a scored ball.

4. Player loses game if he commits three *successive fouls.* If more than a two-player game, balls previously pocketed by disqualified player remain off the table.

5. When a skilled player has the *cue ball in hand behind the head string* (as after a *scratch*) and the legal object ball is also behind the head string, the object ball may be spotted on the foot spot at his request.

6. When a less skilled player has the cue ball in hand behind the head string (as after a scratch) and all of the object balls are also behind the head string, the object ball nearest the head string may be spotted at his request. If two or more object balls are an equal distance from the head string, he may also designate which of the equidistant object balls he desires to be spotted.

ILLEGALLY POCKETED BALLS: All spotted; no penalty.

OBJECT BALLS JUMPED OFF THE TABLE: All spotted. The stroke is a foul, and the player's inning ends. The penalty for fouls is followed.

CUE BALL AFTER JUMPING OFF THE TABLE OR SCRATCH: Incoming player has cue ball in hand behind the head string.

PENALTY FOR FOULS: No point penalty. If foul is other than jumped cue ball or cue ball scratch, incoming player accepts the cue ball in position. A third consecutive foul by the same player is loss of game.

———— PEA (KELLY) POOL ————

Except when clearly contradicted by these additional rules,
the **General Rules of Pocket Billiards** apply.

TYPE OF GAME: **Pea** (or Kelly) **Pool** is an old favorite among pocket billiard players who enjoy a group game in which the competitors play individually, and which entails a bit of luck (not so much in the actual play but rather in the *pea* or *pill* each player receives during each game). The game is very popular since it can accommodate players of widely differing levels of ability.

PLAYERS: 2 or more, with the best game being from four to six.

BALLS USED: Standard set of object balls numbered 1-15, plus *cue ball*. A set of fifteen number peas (or "pills") and a *shake bottle* are also used.

THE RACK: Standard *triangle* rack with 1-ball on the *foot spot,* 2-ball on racker's right corner, 3-ball on left corner. All other balls placed at random.

DETERMINING PRIVATE NUMBERS: After the balls are racked, but before play begins, each player is given a pea from the shake bottle (containing the peas numbered 1-15). The number of the pea is the player's private number and is kept secret.

OBJECT OF THE GAME: To legally pocket the object ball with the numerical value equivalent to the player's private number.

SCORING: No point value for object balls except the ball equivalent to pocketing player's private number; when a player legally pockets that object ball, he wins the game. **Option:** Game is played until a player legally pockets "his own" ball and wins, as above; he receives two points from each player for winning the game. In addition when any player's "private number ball" is legally pocketed by any player other than himself, the pocketing player receives one point and the player whose ball was pocketed loses one point. Players whose private number balls have been pocketed by other players continue to shoot in the regular rotation, but if a player fails to announce that his object ball was pocketed by another player prior to a subsequent shot is being taken, the offending player is disqualified from further play during the game, and the forfeiture of points to the pocketing player is increased from one to two. If no player succeeds in pocketing his private number ball, the game ends when the last private number ball is pocketed, and another game is played with all point values doubled and player who pocketed the last private number ball being the starting player.

OPENING BREAK: Starting player must make an *open break*. If he fails to do so, incoming player has choice of either (1) *cue ball in hand behind the head string* and *table in position,* or (2) having the balls reracked and shooting the opening break shot himself.

RULES OF PLAY:

1. A legally pocketed ball entitles shooter to continue at the table until he fails to legally pocket a ball.

2. On all shots, the cue ball's first contact must be with the lowest-numbered object ball on the table and then must either (1) pocket a ball, or (2) cause the cue ball or any object ball to contact a *cushion*. Failure to do so is a *foul*.

3. A player legally pocketing a ball must shoot again. He may not call a *safety* and *spot* a pocketed ball.

4. When a player has the cue ball in hand behind the head string (as after a *scratch*) and the legal object ball is also behind the head string, the object ball may be spotted on the foot spot at his request.

ILLEGALLY POCKETED BALLS: All spotted; no penalty.

OBJECT BALLS JUMPED OFF THE TABLE: All spotted. The stroke is a foul, and the penalty for fouls is followed.

CUE BALL AFTER JUMP OR SCRATCH: Incoming player has cue ball in hand behind the head string.

PENALTY FOR FOULS: No point penalty. Incoming player has choice of either (1) accepting the table in position and shooting, or (2) requiring offending player to shoot again (if cue ball is in hand behind the string, it is so for either player).

—— POKER POCKET BILLIARDS ——

Except when clearly contradicted by these additional rules,
the **General Rules of Pocket Billiards** apply.

THE GAME: **Poker Pocket Billiards** is played with a white cue ball and a special set of sixteen object balls.

Fifteen of the object balls are numbered from 1 to 15, while the sixteenth ball has a "J" marked on two sides. Three of the numbered balls are also marked with a "J", which represents a "Jack," as in poker played with cards.

Four of the numbered balls are marked with an "A" for ace; four are marked with a "K" for king, and the remaining four are marked with a "Q" for queen.

START OF GAME: Rotation of play may be determined by lag or lot. The object balls are racked in any order on the foot spot in a 16-ball rectangle. (See Diagram 12.) Starting player has cue ball in hand.

SCORING: The object of the game is to get a better poker hand than your opponents. The best hand is four of a kind–four aces, for example. The next best hand is a full house; then three of a kind; then two pairs; then a straight (ace, king, queen, jack) and finally a pair (two of a kind).

No player is allowed to score more than five balls in a single inning. Balls pocketed legally remain off the table.

THE BREAK: Starting player is credited with all balls scored on the break shot, providing he doesn't foul. If he counts, he continues shooting until he misses or pockets the limit of five balls allowed in one inning.

Poker Pocket Billiards

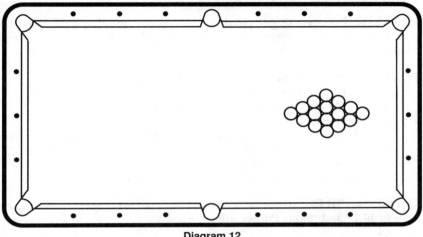

Diagram 12

INCOMING PLAYER: Incoming player accepts balls in position and is limited to five scores in a single inning.

NUMBER OF PLAYERS: Two or more players can play.

GAME ENDS: Game ends when all the balls have been legally pocketed. For example, one player may have five balls to his credit. Another may have three scores. A third player may have four balls in his "hand." A fourth player may have two counts. In this event, two object balls remain on the table. The player with five balls to his credit can continue to shoot in turn, spotting a ball from his hand each time he pockets a ball. He continues to pocket and spot balls in an attempt to better his hand, until he misses or scores the limit of five balls in an inning. The player with four counts to his credit, shooting in turn, can pocket a fifth ball and continue to shoot for the lone ball on the table in an effort to better his hand, spotting a ball each time he pockets one. He continues until he misses.

A player with three balls to his credit, however, with only two object balls on the table, ends the game if he pockets the two balls. In other words, he doesn't spot a ball after scoring, since he has only five counts to his credit.

ORDER OF FINISH: When all the balls are pocketed to end the game, players make the best poker hand out of the balls to their credit. A player with only three balls—if, for example, they are three kings—would win over a player who has five scores, but can get only two pairs out of this hand.

A player with one ball to his credit defeats a player with no counts.

A player with no balls to his credit finishes ahead of a player with no counts, who owes a ball as the result of a foul.

DELIBERATE MISS: It is obvious that if a player, who has five balls to his credit, cannot better his hand by pocketing the balls on the table, he will miss deliberately rather than pocket a ball that will not better his hand. In making a deliberate miss, player must drive an object ball to a cushion or cause the cue ball to hit a cushion after striking an object ball. Failure is a foul.

PENALTIES: Players are penalized one ball for each foul. If a player fouls with no balls to his credit, he owes one to the table. If a player is forced to spot a ball from his hand as the result of a foul, he can choose the ball he wants to spot.

FOULS: A player has fouled in Poker Pocket Billiards when:
1. He fails to hit an object ball.
2. Drives the cue ball or any object ball off the table.
3. Fails to have one foot on the floor when stroking.
4. Touches the cue ball except with the tip of the cue on a legitimate stroke or touches any object ball on the table, except on legal contact by the cue ball.
5. Fails to comply with rule on "deliberate miss." (Above.)

GENERAL RULES: When not in conflict with specific game provisions, the rules of **14.1 Continuous Pocket Billiards** apply.

WILD GAMES: 1. By agreement, players can make the "J" ball "wild," players pocketing the "J's" designating them as any "card" they wish when the "hands are laid down" at the conclusion of the game. For example, a player with three "A" balls (aces) and a "J" ball (jack, which is wild) can call his hand "four aces."

2. Players may draw a ball from the shake bottle, the number of which is kept secret from all the players until the game is over. At the conclusion of the game, the secret number is revealed. If, for example, the number corresponds to a "K" ball, all the kings are wild, players holding kings thus having the advantage of a wild card in finally calling their hands.

3. Each player can draw a number from the shake bottle, which makes all balls he scores of that number wild.

———— SIX BALL ————

Except when clearly contradicted by these additional rules,
the **General Rules of Pocket Billiards** apply.

TYPE OF GAME: Six Ball is a variation of **Rotation** in which the lowest-numbered ball on the table must always be the player's first cue ball contact. If a player complies, any pocketed ball counts. For example, if a player strikes the 1-ball legally, which then caroms into the 6-ball and causes it to be pocketed, that player wins the game. It's fast, and with only six object balls on the table, single inning racks are very common!

PLAYERS: 2 or more, though 2 players are generally preferred.

BALLS USED: Object balls 1-6, plus *cue ball.*

THE RACK: Triangle rack (rows of 1-2-3) with the 1-ball on the *foot spot,* and the 6-ball in the center of the rear row. All other balls placed entirely at random.

OBJECT OF THE GAME: To legally pocket the 6-ball.

SCORING: The balls have no point value. The player legally pocketing the 6-ball is credited with a game won.

OPENING BREAK: The starting player must (1) make an *open break,* or (2) legally pocket an object ball. If he fails to do so, the incoming player has choice of (1) *cue ball in hand behind the head string* and object balls in position, or (2) having the balls reracked and shooting the opening break shot himself.

RULES OF PLAY:

1. A legal shot requires that the cue ball's first contact be with the lowest-numbered ball on the table. A player must then (1) pocket a ball, or (2) cause the cue ball or any object ball to contact a cushion. Failure to do so is a foul.

2. A legally pocketed ball entitles a shooter to remain at the table until he fails to pocket a ball on a legal shot.

3. When a player legally pockets a ball, he must shoot again. He may not call a *safety* and spot a legally pocketed object ball.

4. It is a loss of game if a player commits three *successive fouls.*

ILLEGALLY POCKETED BALLS: All spotted; no penalty, (Common Option, coin-operated play: None spotted except *game ball.*)

OBJECT BALLS JUMPED OFF THE TABLE: All spotted. The stroke is a foul, and the penalty for fouls is followed.

CUE BALL AFTER JUMPING OFF THE TABLE OR SCRATCH: Incoming player has *cue ball in hand.*

PENALTY FOR FOULS: Incoming player is awarded *cue ball in hand.* However, if a 3rd consecutive foul, Rule of Play 4 provides for a penalty of loss of game.

SNOOKER GAMES

Pocket billiard games in America in the 1800s generally evolved from English Billiards (with two cue balls and one red ball) which was played on a 6x12 foot table with rails that sloped into the pocket openings. By 1860 New York table manufacturer, author and noted player Michael Phelan replaced the sloping sides of the pockets with straight corners, thus changing the direction of American pocket billiards from the English game from that time to the present.

English Billiards could only be played with two players, so eventually multi-player variations such as Life Pool and Pyramid Pool became popular in America, England, and territories in which English soldiers were stationed. Life Pool featured different colored balls used as both cue balls and/or object balls depending on the situation and the number of players. Pyramid Pool featured 15 red balls racked on the Pyramid (foot) Spot, and each player received one point for each red he legally potted. Black Pool was a form of Pyramid Pool which used the black ball from a Life Pool set so that a player could alternately pot a red and then attempt the black for extra points. Legend has it that in 1875, Sir Neville Chamberlain, an English regiment soldier stationed in Jubbulpore, India, was playing Black Pool with his fellow officers when he got the idea to add other colored balls to the game so that the variation eventually featured 15 red balls, a yellow, green, pink and black ball [a blue and brown ball were added some years later]. In the course of play one day a visiting military cadet remarked that first year cadets at his particular academy were known as "snookers." When the cadet missed a particularly easy pot, Chamberlain exclaimed to him, "Why, you're a regular snooker!" After explaining the meaning of the word to his fellow peers, officer Chamberlian added that perhaps they were all snookers at the game. The term was adopted for this particular variation, and the game has been called snooker ever since.

Snooker spread to other posts, and soldiers returning to England introduced the game there. Champion player John Roberts, Jr. learned the rules of the game on one of his exhibition tours of India, and he may have had some influence in further popularizing the game in the UK. When English Billiards started losing spectator interest at professional matches in England in the 1930s, champion billiardist Joe Davis recognized snooker as a more appealing alternative, and his cue prowess at the game eventually led to snooker being embraced as the more popular championship discipline in that country.

Snooker has never gained as much popularity in the U.S., but its appeal to many American players, its rank as the #1 televised sport on English television, and the skillful variations it has bred around the world warrants the inclusion of three pertinent sets of rules in this section.

English Snooker – 6 x 12 Table

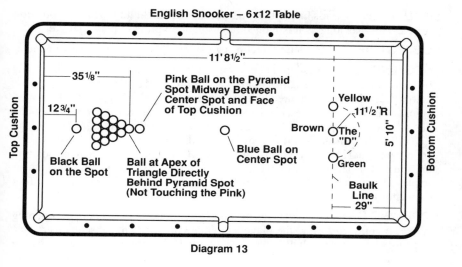

Diagram 13

—— INTERNATIONAL SNOOKER——

TYPE OF GAME: **International** or **"English" Snooker** is the most widely played form of snooker around the world. It is generally played on 6 x 12' English billiard tables, with cushions that are more narrow than on pocket billiard tables and which curve smoothly into the pocket openings. 5 x 10 and snooker tables of even smaller playing dimensions may be used for the game. On a 6 x 12 snooker (English billiard) table the playing area within the cushion faces shall measure 11' 8 1/2" x 5 ' 10" with a tolerance on both dimensions of ± $^1/_2$'.

PLAYERS: 2

BALLS USED: Set of Snooker balls: fifteen object balls that are not numbered and are solid red (called reds), six object balls that may or may not be numbered (called colors) and a cue ball (called the white ball). Point values for object balls: yellow-2, green-3, brown-4, blue-5, pink-6, black-7. In International Snooker the balls used are 2-$^1/_{16}$" diameter.

THE RACK: Play begins with balls placed as in Diagram 13. The pink is spotted on the Pyramid Spot. The apex ball of the triangle of reds is racked as close as possible to the pink without touching it.

BAULK-LINE AND BAULK: A straight line drawn 29" from the face of the *bottom cushion* and parallel to it is called the *Baulk-line* and the intervening space termed the *Baulk*.

THE D: The *D* is a semi-circle described in Baulk with its center at the middle of the Baulk-line and with a radius of 11 1/2". When the *striker* has *cue ball in hand within the D* he may place the base of the cue ball anywhere on the line or within the D, and may use his hand or any part of his cue (including the tip) to position the cue ball—as long as it is judged he is not attempting to play a stroke.

OBJECT OF THE GAME: To score a greater number of points than opponent.

SCORING: Points are scored in two ways: players are awarded points for fouls by the opponent (see "Penalties For Fouls" below), and by legally *potting* reds or colors. Each legally potted red ball has a point value of one; each legally potted color ball has a point value as indicated ("Balls Used" above). A *frame* ends when all balls have been potted, following the Rules of Play; if, however, only the black (7) ball is left on the table, the frame ends with the first score or foul. If the players' scores are equal after that scoring, the black ball is spotted on its original position and the players lag or draw lots for the choice of playing at, or assigning opponent to play at, the black ball with the *cue ball in hand within the D,* first score or foul then ends the frame.

OPENING BREAK: Players lag or draw lots for choice of break in the opening frame. In a match format the players alternate the break in subsequent frames. Starting player has cue ball in hand within the D. He must cause the cue ball to contact a red ball. It is not necessary to send a ball to a rail or into a pocket. Failure to meet this requirement is a foul (see "Penalties For Fouls"). A foul is scored and —with all fouls —the incoming player has choice of (1) accepting the table and becoming the striker, or (2) requiring offender to break again.

RULES OF PLAY:

1. A legally potted ball entitles the striker to continue at the table until he fails to legally pot a ball.

2. On all shots, the striker must comply with the appropriate requirements of Rules of Play 5 and 6. It is not necessary to cause the cue ball or an object ball to contact a cushion or drop in a pocket after the cue ball has contacted a legal object ball *(ball on).* Failure to contact a legal object ball first is a foul.

3. As long as reds are on the table, the incoming striker (player taking his first stroke of an inning) always has a red as his legal object ball (ball *on*).

4. Any red balls potted on a legal shot are legally potted balls; the striker need not call any particular red ball(s), pocket(s) or details of how the pot will be played.

5. When the striker has a red ball as his "ball on" (legal object ball), he must cause the cue ball's first contact to be with a red ball. Failure to do so is a foul (See "Penalties For Fouls.")

6. After the striker has scored a red ball initially, his next legal object is a color, and as long as reds remain on the table he must alternate his play between reds and colors (though within each group he may play ball of his choice). When reds remain on the table and a color is his object, the striker must (a) designate prior to stroking which color ball is his object (that specific color is then his "ball on"), and (b) cause the cue ball's first contact with a ball to be with that colored ball. If the striker fails to meet these requirements, it is a foul (See "Penalties For Fouls.")

7. If the striker's ball *on* is a red, and he pots a color, it is a foul.

8. If the striker's ball *on* is a color, and he pots any other ball, it is a foul.

9. Jump shots are illegal in International snooker. It is a foul if the striker intentionally causes the cue ball to jump (rise from the bed of the table) by any

means, if the jump is an effort to clear an obstructing ball.

10. While reds remain on the table, each potted color ball is spotted prior to the next stroke (see "Spotting Balls" below for spotting rules). After a color has been spotted, if the striker plays while that ball is incorrectly spotted (and opponent or referee calls it before two such plays have been taken), the shot taken is a foul. If the striker plays two strokes after such error without its being announced by opponent or referee, he is free of penalty and continues playing and scoring normally as though the spotting error simply had not occurred. The striker is responsible for ensuring that all balls are correctly spotted before striking. If the striker plays while a ball(s) that should be on the table is not a foul may be awarded whenever the foul is discovered during the striker's inning. Any scoring prior to the discovery of the foul will count.

11. When no reds remain on the table, striker's balls *on* become the colors, in ascending numerical order (2,3,4,5,6,7). These legally potted colors are not spotted after each is potted; they remain off the table. (The black (7) ball is an exception in the case of a tie score; see "Scoring.")

ILLEGALLY POTTED BALL: Reds illegally potted are not spotted; they remain off the table. Colors illegally potted are spotted. (See "Spotting Balls.")

OBJECT BALLS JUMPED OFF THE TABLE: Reds jumped off the table are not spotted and the striker has committed a foul. Colors jumped off the table are spotted and the striker has committed a foul. (See "Penalties For Fouls.")

SPOTTING BALLS: Reds are never spotted. Colors to be spotted are placed as at the start of the game. If a color's spot is occupied (to mean that to spot it would make it touch a ball), it is placed on the spot of the highest value color that is unoccupied. If all spots are occupied, the color is spotted as close as possible to its original spot on a straight line between its spot and the nearest point on the *top* (foot) cushion.

CUE BALL AFTER JUMPING OFF THE TABLE: Incoming player has cue ball in hand within the D. When cue ball is in hand within the D (except on the opening break), there is no restriction (based on position of reds or colors) as to what balls may be played; striker may play at any ball *on* regardless of where it is on the table.

TOUCHING A BALL: While balls are in play it is a foul if the striker touches any object ball or if the striker touches the cue ball with anything other than the cue tip during a legal stroke.

SNOOKERED: The cue ball is *snookered* when a direct stroke in a straight line to any part of every ball *on* is obstructed by a ball or balls not *on*. If there is any one ball that is not so obstructed, the cue ball is not snookered. If in-hand within the D, the cue ball is snookered only if obstructed from all positions on or within the D. If the cue ball is obstructed by more than one ball, the one nearest to the cue ball is the effective snookering ball.

ANGLED: The cue ball is *angled* when a direct stroke in a straight line to any part of every ball *on* is obstructed by a corner of the cushion. If there is any one ball *on* that is not so obstructed, the cue ball is not angled. If angled after a foul the referee or player will state "Angled Ball," and the striker has the choice to either (1) play from that position or (2) play from in hand within the D.

OCCUPIED: A spot is said to be occupied if a ball cannot be placed on it without its touching another ball.

TOUCHING BALL: If the cue ball is touching another ball which is, or can be, *on* , the referee or player shall state "Touching Ball." Thereafter the striker must play away from it or it is a push stroke (foul). No penalty is incurred for thus playing away if (1) the ball is not *on*; the ball is *on* and the striker nominates such ball; or (3) the ball is *on* and the striker nominates, and first hits, another ball. [If the referee considers that a touching ball has moved through an agency other than the player, it is not a foul.]

PUSH STROKE: A push stroke is a foul and is made when the tip of the cue remains in contact with the cue ball (1) when the cue ball makes contact with the object ball, or (2) after the cue ball has commenced its forward motion. Provided that where the cue ball and an object ball are almost touching, it shall be deemed a legal stroke if the cue ball hits the finest possible edge of the object ball.

MISS: The striker shall to the best of his ability endeavor to hit the ball *on*. If the referee considers the rule infringed he shall call foul and "miss." The incoming player (1) may play the ball(s) as they lie, or (2) may request that the ball(s) be returned to the original position and have the offending player play the stroke again. Note: if the ball *on* cannot possibly be hit, the striker is judged to be attempting to hit the ball *on*.

FREE BALL: After a foul, if the cue ball is snookered, the referee or player shall state *"Free Ball."* If the non-offending player takes the next stroke he may nominate *any* ball as *on*. For this stroke, such ball shall be regarded as, and acquire the value of, the ball *on*. It is a foul should the cue ball fail to first hit, or - except when only pink and black remain on the table be snookered by, the *free ball*. If the "free ball" is potted, it is spotted, and the value of the ball *on* is scored. If the ball *on* is potted it is scored. If both the "free ball" and the ball *on* are potted, only the value of the ball *on* is scored.

FOULS: If a foul is committed:

1. the player who committed the foul incurs the penalty prescribed (which is added to the opponent's score), and has to play again if requested by the next player. Once such a request has been made it cannot be withdrawn.

2. should more than one foul be committed in the same stroke the highest value penalty shall be incurred.

3. any ball improperly spotted shall remain where positioned, except that if off the table it shall be correctly spotted.

PENALTIES FOR FOULS: The following are fouls and incur a penalty of four points or the higher one prescribed:
1. value of the ball *on* -
    by striking
        a. when the balls are still moving from the previous shot.
        b. the cue ball more than once (double hit).
        c. without at least one foot on the floor.
        d. out of turn.
        e. improperly from in hand within the D.
    by causing
        f. the cue ball to miss all object balls.
        g. the cue ball to enter a pocket.
        h. a snooker with free ball.
        i. a jump shot.

2. value of the ball *on* or ball concerned -
    by causing
        a. a ball not *on* to enter a pocket.
        b. the cue ball to first hit a ball not *on*.
        c. a push stroke.
        d. by striking with a ball not correctly spotted.
        e. by touching a ball with other than the tip of the cue.
        f. by forcing a ball off the table.

3. value of the ball *on* or higher value of the two balls by causing the cue ball to hit simultaneously two balls other than two reds or a "free ball" and the ball *on*.

4. penalty of seven points is incurred if -
    the striker
        a. after potting a red commits a foul before nominating a color.
        b. uses a ball off the table for any purpose.
        c. plays at reds in successive strokes.
        d. uses as the cue ball any ball other than the white one.

———— AMERICAN SNOOKER ————

TYPE OF GAME: American Snooker is a "cousin" of Snooker as it is played widely around the world, the rules giving it a distinct orientation toward the structure of many American pocket billiard games. It is generally played on either 5 x 10 or 6 x 12 Snooker tables, with cushions that are more narrow than other pocket billiard tables, and curve smoothly into the pocket openings. The balls used are either 2-^{1}/$_{16}$" or 2-^{1}/$_8$" diameter. (See **BCA Specifications**.)

PLAYERS: 2.

BALLS USED: Set of Snooker balls: fifteen object balls that are not numbered and are solid red (called reds), six object balls that may or may not be numbered (called colors) and a cue ball. Point values for object balls: yellow-2, green-3, brown-4, blue-5, pink-6, black-7.

THE RACK: Play begins with balls placed as in Diagram 14.

OBJECT OF THE GAME: To score a greater number of points than opponent.

SCORING: Points are scored in two ways; players are awarded points for fouls by the opponent (see "Penalty For Foul" below), and by legally pocketing reds or colors. Each legally pocketed red ball has a point value of one; each legally pocketed color ball has a point value as indicated ("Balls Used" above). Game ends when all balls have been pocketed, following the Rules of Play; if, however, only the black (7) ball is left on the table, the game ends with the first score or foul. If the players' scores are equal after that scoring, the black ball is spotted on its original position and the players lag for the choice of shooting at, or assigning opponent to shoot at the black ball with the *cue ball in hand within the D;* the first score or foul then ends the game.

American Snooker – 5x10 Table

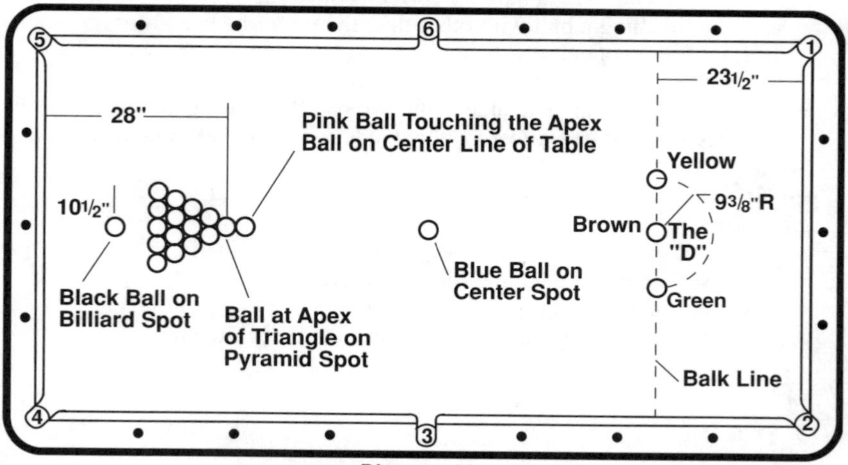

Pink Ball Touching the Apex Ball on Center Line of Table

28"

10 1/2"

Black Ball on Billiard Spot

Ball at Apex of Triangle on Pyramid Spot

Blue Ball on Center Spot

23 1/2"

Yellow

9 3/8"R

Brown   The "D"

Green

Balk Line

Diagram 14

OPENING BREAK: Starting player has cue ball in hand within the D. He must (1) cause the cue ball to contact a red ball prior to contacting a color, and (2) cause a red ball to contact a cushion or drop into a pocket, and (3) cause the cue ball to contact a cushion after it contacts a red ball. Failure to meet these requirements is a foul and a *breaking violation.* A foul is scored and incoming player has choice of (1) accepting the table and shooting, or (2) requiring offender to break again.

RULES OF PLAY:

1. A legally pocketed ball entitles shooter to continue at the table until he fails to legally pocket a ball.

2. On all shots, player must comply with the appropriate requirements of Rules of Pay 5 and 6, plus cause the cue ball or an object ball to contact a cushion or drop in a pocket after the cue ball has contacted a legal object ball (on ball). Failure to do so is a foul.

3. As long as reds are on the table, an incoming player (player taking his first shot of an inning) always has a red as his legal object ball (on ball).

4. Any red balls pocketed on a legal shot are legally pocketed balls; player need not call any particular red ball(s), pocket(s) or mode of pocketing.

5. When a player has a red ball as his "on ball" (required legal object ball), he must cause the cue ball's first contact to be with a red ball. Failure to do so is a foul. Rule of Play 2 also applies.

6. After a player has scored a red ball initially, his next legal object is a color, and as long as reds remain on the table he must alternate his play between reds and colors (though within each group he may play ball of his choice). When reds remain on the table and a color is his object, the player must (a) designate prior to shooting which color ball is his object (that specific color is then his "on ball"), and (b) cause the cue ball's first contact with a ball to be with that color ball. If player fails to meet these requirements, it is a foul. Rule #2 requirements also apply.

7. If player's on ball is a red and he pockets a color, it is a foul.

8. If player's on ball is a color and he pockets any other ball, it is a foul.

9. It is a foul if a player intentionally causes the cue ball to jump (rise from the bed of the table) by any means, if the jump is an effort to clear an obstructing ball.

10. While reds remain on the table, each pocketed color ball is spotted prior to the next stroke. (See "Spotting Balls" below for spotting rules.) If player shooting after a color has been spotted plays while that ball is incorrectly spotted (and opponent or referee calls it before two such shots have been taken), the shot taken is a foul. If such shooting player shoots twice after such error without its being announced by opponent or referee, he is free of penalty and continues shooting and scoring normally as though the spotting error simply had not occurred.

11. When no reds remain on the table, player's on balls become the colors, in ascending numerical order (2, 3, 4, 5, 6, 7). These legally pocketed colors are not spotted after each is pocketed; they remain off the table (the seven-ball is an exception in the case of a tie score; see "Scoring.")

ILLEGALLY POCKETED BALL: Reds illegally pocketed are not spotted; they remain off the table. Colors illegally pocketed are spotted (See "Spotting Balls.")

OBJECT BALLS JUMPED OFF THE TABLE: Reds jumped off the table are not spotted. Colors jumped off the table are spotted. The stroke is a foul, and the penalty for fouls is followed.

SPOTTING BALLS: Reds are never spotted. Colors to be spotted are placed as at the start of the game. If a color's spot is occupied (to mean that to spot it would make it touch a ball), it is placed on the spot of the highest value color that is unoccupied. If all spots are occupied, the color is spotted as close as possible to its original spot on a straight line between its spot and the nearest point on the foot cushion.

CUE BALL AFTER JUMPING OFF THE TABLE OR SCRATCH: Incoming player has cue ball in hand within the D. When cue ball is in hand within the D (except on the opening break), there is no restriction (based on position of reds or colors) as to what balls may be played; player may play at an on ball regardless of where it is on the table.

PENALTY FOR FOULS: Seven points are added to non-fouling player's score for each foul committed (no deduction from offender's score). Incoming (non-offending) player has the choice of either (1) accepting the table in position and shooting, or (2) requiring the offending player to shoot again; if the foul is a cue ball jumped off the table or a cue ball scratch, the cue ball is in hand within the D for either player. If the foul is other than cue ball jumped off the table or scratch, the cue ball remains in position.

GOLF

TYPE OF GAME: In many sections of the United States the most popular game on a snooker table is Golf. It is usually played on a 5 x 10 ' or 6 x 12 ' snooker table with either 2-¹/₈ " or 2-¹/₁₆ " diameter snooker balls. (See **BCA Specifications.**)

PLAYERS: 2 or more, with a game often including 4 players or more.

BALLS USED: The numbered group of snooker balls (2-Yellow thru 7-black) and a white snooker cue ball.

THE RACK: Starting player's object ball is spotted on the foot (*pyramid*) spot.

OBJECT OF THE GAME: For a player to successfully pocket his object ball in each of the six pockets in numerical pocket order (Diagram 14) before his opponent(s) does.

DETERMINING ORDER OF PLAY: Players draw lots (or numbered peas) from a shake bottle. Lowest-drawn number goes first with the remainder of the order corresponding to the ascending draw of peas for each player. Starting player's object ball throughout the game is the 2-ball (yellow); the next player—the 3-ball (green); the next player—the 4-ball (brown); etc.

SCORING: The balls have no numerical value for scoring. The first player to follow the rules of play and legally pocket his object ball in the #6 (side) pocket wins the game. Players keep track of the number of fouls (known as hickeys) each competitor accrues throughout the game. A *hickey* may be assigned any value, and players must determine the differences in the totals of hickeys due at the end of each game. For example, if the winning Player A has 6 hickeys, Player B has 4 hickeys, and Player C has 10 hickeys, Player A's hickeys are irrelevant. Player B owes Player A the value of 4 hickeys and Player C owes Player A the value of 10 hickeys. Usually the game itself has a value and Player A receives that value from each player for winning the game.

OPENING BREAK: Starting player begins play with the cue ball on or within the D and his object ball (for the starting player—the yellow 2-ball) on the foot spot. His objective is to pocket his ball in pocket #1. If the first player misses, the second player takes the cue ball in hand within the D positions his object ball (3—the green) on the foot spot and attempts to pocket it in pocket #1. If the second player misses, the third player takes cue ball in hand within the D, positions his object ball (4—the brown) on the foot spot, and attempts to pocket it in pocket #1. Subsequent players follow the same procedure to enter the game. If a player pockets his first shot into pocket #1, his object ball is re-spotted on the foot spot and the player shoots again to pocket his object ball in pocket #2 from wherever the cue ball comes to rest. Once his inning is complete, the next player entering the game takes cue ball in hand within the D and starts play as described above.

SUBSEQUENT HOLES: After all players have entered the game (unless a player runs out the game from his break) the cue ball is played from wherever it comes to rest after each player's shot for the remainder of the game (See below if jumped or scratched.) Once a player pockets his object ball in pocket #1, the object ball is re-spotted on the foot spot, and the player continues shooting for pocket #2. When he misses, the next player shoots at his object ball. A player must successfully complete all six holes, playing in order, in this manner. The player who completes this pattern first wins the game.

RULES OF PLAY:

1. It is a foul to pocket the object ball in any pocket other than the one in which the player is attempting to score.

2. On all shots it is necessary for the player to hit his object ball first.

3. To be a legal shot, a player is required to either send the cue ball to a rail and then hit his object ball first, hit his object ball first and pocket it, or hit his object ball first and send any ball to a cushion.

4. It is a foul to strike, touch or in any way make contact with the cue ball in play or any object balls in play with anything (the body, clothing, chalk, mechanical bridge, cue shaft, etc.) **except** the cue tip (while attached to the cue shaft), which may contact the cue ball in the execution of a legal shot.

5. It is a foul to hit another player's object ball first. If a player hits an opponent's object ball first, the player loses his turn, is credited with a hickey, and the opponent has the choice of returning the object ball to its original position.

6. If a player has a clear shot at his full object ball and misses the entire ball, it is a foul (hickey), he loses his turn, and the object ball is spotted on the foot spot.

7. If a player commits a foul and the incoming player is snookered from seeing his entire ball, that player may mark the position(s) of the offending ball(s), remove the obstacle ball (s) from the table, shoot at his object ball, and replace the removed ball(s) to original position(s) immediately after the stroke.

ILLEGALLY POCKETED BALLS: All are spotted on the foot spot, unless an opponent's ball was struck first. Then the opponent may choose to return his object ball to its original position. The stroke is a foul and the offending player receives a hickey.

OBJECT BALLS JUMPED OFF THE TABLE: An object ball that jumps off the table is a foul, and the offending player loses his turn and receives a hickey. The object ball is spotted on the foot spot unless an opponent's ball was struck first. In that case the opponent may choose to return his object ball to its original position.

CUE BALL AFTER JUMPING OFF THE TABLE OR SCRATCH: The offending player fouls, loses his turn, and receives a hickey. The incoming player has cue ball in hand on or within the D, may shoot in any direction, and may shoot at his object ball if it is in the D as well. Any object balls pocketed on the foul stroke are re-spotted on the foot spot in numerical order unless an opponent's ball was struck first. In that case the opponent may choose to return his object ball to its original position.

SPOTTING BALLS: After each player has completed his opening break shot, if a player is required to spot a ball on the foot spot, he must do so immediately after the resulting stroke. If the ball cannot be spotted without touching another ball, the ball is spotted as close to it as possible without touching (if the obstacle ball is the cue ball) and frozen to the ball (if the obstacle ball is an object ball), and on the direct line between the foot spot and the foot rail.

GENERAL RULES OF CAROM BILLIARDS

The rules in this section apply generally to all the specific forms and varieties of carom billiard games included in this rulebook. Certain games, however, do have exceptions that supersede or modify the General Rules; these exceptions are flagged with a parenthetical notation, referencing the particular game or variation in which the general rule might be either modified or nonapplicable. Thus, unless specifically noted otherwise, these General Rules apply to all carom billiard games.

To facilitate the use and understanding of these General Rules, many terms that may require definition for some readers are set in italic in their first appearance, so that the reader may refer to the **Glossary of Billiard Terms** section for the exact meaning of the term.

For purposes of simplicity and clarity, masculine pronouns have been utilized throughout this rulebook. Obviously, such references should be considered to apply to any player, regardless of gender.

Although most references in these rules are to a "player" or "players"; since most carom billiard games can be adapted to team play, the reader should interpret the rules as equally applicable to a team of teams when appropriate.

The United States Billiard Association today sanctions most U.S. play of the popular carom game of **Three-Cushion Billiards.** In the individual game rules for Three-Cushion, the U.S.B.A. official rules have been reprinted exactly as published by that group, resulting in some duplication of General Rules from this section within U.S.B.A.'s rules.

TABLES, BALL, EQUIPMENT. All games are contested on tables, and with balls and equipment, meeting the standards prescribed in the **BCA Specifications.**

The Carom Table

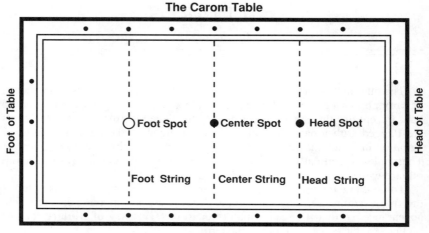

Diagram 15

BALLS DEFINED. Two white balls and a red; each player has a white ball that is a cue ball when he is shooting, while the red is never a cue ball. One of the white balls has two or three small colored spots to differentiate it from the other. (**Note: Four Ball** is played with a fourth ball as well; see **Four Ball** rules.)

STRIKING CUE BALL. Legal shots require that the *cue ball* only be struck with the *cue tip* only.

DETERMINING FIRST PLAYER. The player to perform the *opening break* shot is determined by either *lag for break* or *lot.* (The lag-for-break procedure is required for formal competition.) The player winning the lag or lot has the choice of performing the opening break shot or assigning it to the opposition.

LAG FOR BREAK. Red ball is spotted on *foot spot* (except in *Four Ball*). With the *cue balls in hand behind the head string,* one player to the right and one to the left of the *head spot,* the balls are shot to the foot *cushion* and back to the head end of the table. The player whose ball ends up closest to the head cushion wins the lag, subject to the following qualifications:

The lagged ball must contact the foot cushion at least once; other cushion contacts are immaterial except as prohibited below. It is an automatic loss of the lag if (1) the ball crosses into the opponent's half of the table, or (2) the ball fails to contact the foot cushion, or (3) the ball jumps the table, or (4) the ball hits the red ball.

If both players violate automatic-loss lag rules as above, or if the referee is unable to determine which ball is closer, the lag is a tie and is replayed.

The lag for opening break is performed by both players simultaneously, although they need not stroke the lag shots in perfect unison.

CHOICE OF CUE BALLS. The winner of the lag has the choice of cue balls, either the all-white "clear" or the color-marked "spot," which is then used throughout the game. If an odd number of players are competing, the same cue ball is **not** played throughout the game. Rather, incoming player always plays the cue ball that was **not** used by the player who immediately preceded him (Exception: **Four Ball Caroms**).

BALL POSITIONS – OPENING BREAK. The red ball is spotted on the foot spot. Non-breaking player's cue ball is spotted on the *head spot*. Breaking player's cue ball is placed on the *head string* within six inches (measured to the ball's center) of the head spot. (Note: **Four Ball** uses a different opening break position.)

The Break Shot

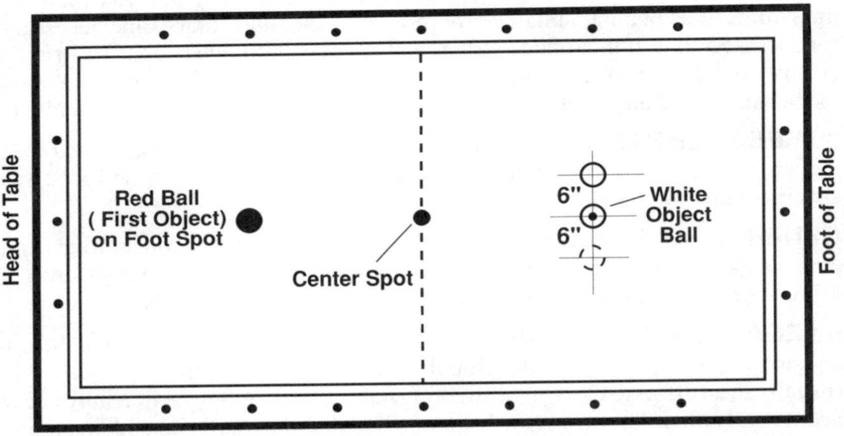

Red Ball
(First Object)
on Foot Spot

Center Spot

6"
6"
White
Object
Ball

Head of Table

Foot of Table

Diagram 16

RED BALL FIRST OBJECT. Player making opening break shot must contact the red ball first, rather than the opponent's cue ball. If the cue ball on the opening break strikes the other white ball first rather than the red ball, it is an *error* and ends his *inning*; no score is valid. (Exception: **Four Ball Caroms**.)

On all subsequent shots, players may make either the red or the white (or "pink" in **Four Ball**) ball his first object (first ball struck by the cue ball). (Exception: **Red Ball**.)

FOOT ON FLOOR. It is a foul if a player shoots when at least one foot is not in contact with the floor. Foot attire must be normal in regard to size, shape and the manner in which it is worn.

SHOOTING WITH BALLS IN MOTION. It is a foul if a player shoots while the cue ball or any object ball is in motion. (A spinning ball is in motion.)

COMPLETION OF STROKE. A stroke is not (complete and therefore is not counted) until all balls on the table have become motionless after the stroke. (A spinning ball is in motion.)

FOULS BY TOUCHING BALLS. It is a foul to strike, touch or in any way make contact with the cue ball in play or any object balls in play with anything (the body, clothing, chalk, *mechanical bridge, cue shaft*,etc.) **except** the cue tip (while attached to the cue shaft), which may contact the cue ball once in the execution of a shot.

FOULS BY DOUBLE HITS. It is a foul if the cue ball is struck more than once on a shot by the cue tip. If, in the referee's judgement, the cue ball has left initial contact with the cue tip and then is struck a second time in the course of the same stroke, it shall be a foul. If the referee judges, by virtue of sound, ball position and action, and stroke used, that there were two separate contacts of the cue ball by the cue tip on a stroke, the stroke is a foul and must be so-called.

PUSH SHOT FOULS. It is a foul if the cue ball is pushed or shoved by the cue tip, with contact being maintained for more than the momentary time necessary for a stroked shot. If the referee judges that the player put the cue tip against the cue ball and then pushed or shoved on into the shot, maintaining contact beyond the normal momentary split-second, the stroke is a foul and must be so-called.

JUMPED CUE BALL. When a stroke results in the cue ball being a *jumped ball*, the stroke is a foul. (Note: jumped object balls may or may not be fouls; see specific game rules.)

GENERAL RULE, ALL FOULS. Though the penalties for fouls differ from game to game, the following applies to all fouls: (1) player's inning ends, and (2) if on a stroke, the stroke is invalid and cannot be a scoring stroke.

ILLEGAL JUMPING OF BALL. It is a foul if a player strikes the cue ball below center ("digs under" it) and **intentionally** causes it to rise off the bed of the table (usually in an effort to clear an obstructing ball). Such jumping action may occur accidentally on occasion, and such "jumps" are not necessarily considered fouls; they may still be ruled foul strokes however, if for example, the ferrule or cue shaft makes contact with the cue ball in the course of the shot.

SPECIAL INTENTIONAL FOUL PENALTY. The cue ball in play shall not be **intentionally** struck with anything other than a cue's attached tip (such as the ferrule, shaft, etc.). While such contact is automatically a foul under the provisions of "Fouls By Touching Balls," if the referee deems the contact to be intentional, he shall warn the player **once** during a match that a second violation during that match will result in the loss of the match by forfeiture, If a second violation does occur, the match must be forfeited.

BALLS MOVING SPONTANEOUSLY. If a ball shifts, settles, turns or otherwise moves "by itself," the ball shall remain in the position it assumed and play continues.

PLAYER RESPONSIBILITY FOULS. The player is responsible for chalk, bridges, files and any other items or equipment he brings to, uses at, or causes to approximate the table. If he drops a pen or a piece of chalk, or knocks off a mechanical bridge head, as examples, he is guilty of a foul should such an object make contact with a ball in play.

JUMPED BALLS DEFINED. Balls coming to rest other than on the bed *of the table* after a stroke (on the cushion top, rail surface, floor, etc.) are considered jumped balls. Balls may bounce on the cushion tops, rails or light fixtures of the table in play without being jumped balls **if** they return to the bed of the table under their own power and without touching anything not a part of the table equipment. The table equipment shall consist of its light fixture, and any permanent parts of the table proper. (Balls that strike or touch anything not a part of the table equipment shall be considered jumped balls even though they might return to the bed of the table after contact with the non-equipment item[s]).

All jumped balls are spotted when all balls have stopped moving. (See "Spotting Jumped Balls.")

OUTSIDE INTERFERENCE. If the balls are moved (or a player bumped such that play is directly affected) by a non-player during a match, the balls shall be replaced as near as possible to their original positions immediately prior to the incident, and play shall resume with no penalty on the player affected. If the match is officiated, the referee shall replace the balls. This rule shall also apply to "act of God" interference, such as earthquake, hurricane, light fixture falling, a power failure, etc.

DEFINITION OF LEGAL SAFETY. Player must drive an object ball to a cushion or cause the cue ball to contact a cushion after striking an object ball. Failure to do so is a foul. (Note: U.S.B.A. Three-Cushion rules prohibit all **intentional** safeties.)

LIMIT ON SAFETY PLAY. Player may not play safety in consecutive innings. When a player's last shot was a safety, he must not play another safety on his next shot. If he does so, it is a foul. (Note: does not apply in U.S.B.A. Three-Cushion play.)

PLAYING FROM SAFETY. When a player has either fouled or played an intentional safety on his last shot, he comes to the table for his next shot "playing from safety."

Player must make an obvious and legal attempt to score. If he again resorts to safety play, whether or not the effort meets the requirements of a legal safety, he has fouled. (Note: "Playing From Safety" does not apply in Three-Cushion.)

SPOTTING JUMPED BALLS. If the cue ball is jumped off the table (foul), is spotted on the head spot (if occupied, the foot spot; if that is also occupied; the center spot).

If the white object ball is jumped, it is spotted on the head spot (if occupied, the foot spot; if that is also occupied, the center spot).

If the red object ball is jumped, it is spotted on the foot spot (if occupied, the head spot; if that is also occupied, the center spot). If the cue ball and an object ball are both jumped, the cue ball is spotted first, then the object ball following the appropriate spotting order above.

If both object balls are jumped, they are spotted as above. If the cue ball occupies either of the object balls' primary spot locations, spot first the ball that spots freely; then the other according to the appropriate alternative spotting order above.

─── CUSHION CAROMS ───

Except when clearly contradicted by these additional rules,
the **General Rules of Carom Billiards** apply.

PLAYERS: 2 or 3.

BALLS USED: Standard set of one white clear, one white spot, and one red.

OBJECT OF THE GAME: Score the predetermined number of points (may be 30-60 in tournament play, or any agreed upon number) for game prior to opponent(s).

SCORING: Each legal *count* is scored as one point for shooter.

DEFINITION OF A COUNT: A shot is a count if not in violation of any "Rules of Play" or **General Rules of Carom Billiards**, and the cue ball contacts both object balls.

OPENING BREAK: General Rules of Carom Billiards regarding opening break apply, as well as "Rule of Play 2" below. Failure to comply is a violation; player's *inning* ends and no count can be scored.

RULES OF PLAY:

1. A legal counting stroke entitles shooter to continue at the table until he fails to legally count on a shot.

2. On all shots, player must cause the cue ball to either (1) contact one or more cushions before contacting object balls, or (2) contact an object ball directly and then one or more cushions before it contacts second object ball. Failure to comply is a violation; player's inning ends and no count can be scored on the violating stroke.

PENALTY FOR FOULS: One point is deducted from offender's score for each *foul*.

─── FOUR BALL CAROMS ───

Except when clearly contradicted by these additional rules,
the **General Rules of Carom Billiards** apply.

PLAYERS: 2.

BALLS USED: Standard set of one white clear, one white spot and one red, plus one light red (pink).

OBJECT OF THE GAME: Score the predetermined number of points for game prior to opponent.

SCORING: Each legal two-ball *carom* count is scored as one point for shooter; each legal three-ball carom count is scored as two points for shooter.

DEFINITION OF A COUNT: If not in violation of any "Rules of Play" or **General Rules of Carom Billiards**, a shot is: a two-ball carom *count* if the *cue ball* contacts any two of the three object balls, or a three-ball carom count if the cue ball contacts all three of the object balls.

BALL POSITIONS – OPENING BREAK: The light red (pink) ball is *spotted* on the *foot spot*. The red ball is spotted on the *head spot*. Both balls are in position before the *lag for break*.

OPENING BREAK: The lag for break is actually part of the *opening break*. With the red and pink balls spotted as immediately above, players select cue balls and lag for break as in **General Rules of Carom Billiards** (automatic loss of lag applying to contact with the pink ball as well as the red). When lag is completed, both players' cue balls remain in position; first shot of the game is from this position (if cue ball[s] contacted either red and/or pink object balls – which were spotted – on lag, they are re-spotted prior to first shot of game). Winner of lag has choice of shooting first or assigning first shot to opponent; in either case, cue ball are played from position following lag for break, and each player's cue ball is the one he used for the lag for break. Starting player (first shooter after lag for break) must cause the cue ball's first contact with a ball to be with the pink object ball (on the foot spot). Failure to comply is a violation; player's inning ends and no count can be scored.

RULES OF PLAY:

1. On all shots subsequent to the first shot following the lag, shooter may make his first object (first balls contacted by the cue ball) any of the three object balls.

2. A legal counting stroke entitles shooter to continue at the table until he fails to legally count on a shot.

SPOTTING JUMPED BALLS: (Differs from **General Rules of Carom Billiards**)

If the red ball is jumped off the table, it is spotted on the *head spot*. If the head spot is occupied (spotting a ball on it would result in contact with another ball), the red ball is held off the table until the first time the head spot is vacant at the completion of a shot.

If the pink ball is jumped, it is spotted on the foot spot. If the foot spot is occupied (spotting a ball on it would result in contact with another ball), the pink ball is held off the table until the first time the foot spot is vacant at the completion of a shot.

If the white object ball is jumped, it is spotted on the head spot. If the head spot is occupied, the white object ball is held off the table until the first time the head spot is vacant at the completion of a shot. Should the head spot be occupied after each shot until such time as the white object ball is required as incoming player's cue ball, that ball shall then be spotted on the foot spot; if the foot spot is also occupied, it shall be spotted on the center spot; if the center spot is also occupied, incoming player may place the ball anywhere on the head string, not *frozen* to a ball.

If the white cue ball is jumped, the same rule (immediately above) applies.

If the red ball and the pink balls are jumped on a shot, spot the pink ball first, then the red ball, according to spotting rules for those balls. If neither can be spotted per those rules, spot the pink ball on the center spot and continue holding the red ball off the table until the head spot is vacant per the red spotting ball rule.

If either one of the white balls and one or both of the red balls are jumped on a shot, first spot the white ball per appropriate rule above, then the red ball per appropriate rule (or if both reds, the immediately preceding paragraph).

If both of the white balls and one of the red balls is jumped, spot all balls that will spot directly (beginning with the white object ball, then the white cue ball, then the red). If all jumped balls cannot be spotted directly, spot remaining balls per appropriate rule above.

If all four balls are jumped on a shot, the jumper's cue ball is spotted on the center spot, the red ball on the head spot, the pink on the foot spot, and the incoming player may place his cue ball anywhere on the head string not frozen to the red ball.

Jumped balls result in no penalty unless the player's cue ball is jumped. If player does jump his cue ball off the table, the stroke is invalid and is a foul.

PENALTY FOR FOULS: One point is deducted from offender's score for each foul.

——————— STRAIGHT RAIL ———————

Except when clearly contradicted by these additional rules,
the **General Rules of Carom Billiards** apply.

PLAYERS: 2 or 3.

BALLS USED: Standard set of one white clear, one white spot and one red.

OBJECT OF THE GAME: Score the predetermined number of points for game prior to opponent(s).

SCORING: Each legal *count* is scored as one point for shooter.

DEFINITION OF A COUNT: A shot is a count if not in violation of any "Rules of Play" or **General Rules of Carom Billiards** and the *cue ball* contacts both object balls.

OPENING BREAK: General Rules of Carom Billiards regarding *opening break* apply. Failure to comply is a violation; player's inning ends and no count can be scored

RULES OF PLAY:

A legal counting stroke entitles shooter to continue at the table until he fails to legally count on a shot.

2. When the object balls are in a *crotch*, player may score no more than three successive counts with the balls remaining in the crotch. If three successive in-crotch counts are made, player must, on his next shot, drive at least one object ball out of the crotch. Failure to do so is a violation; players's inning ends and no count can be scored.

PENALTY FOR FOULS: One point is deducted from offender's score for each foul.

—— UNITED STATES BILLIARD —— ASSOCIATION THREE-CUSHION RULES

1. USBA-sanctioned tournaments will be governed by the rules that follow. Any exception must be stated in the tournament notice, or discussed and approved by a majority of the players present before the start of any USBA tournament.

2. A three-cushion billiard is valid and is a count of one in any of the following cases: (1) cue ball strikes an object ball and then strikes three or more cushions before striking the second object ball; (2) cue ball strikes three or more cushions and then strikes the two object balls; (3) cue ball strikes a cushion, then strikes one object ball, and then strikes two or more cushions before striking the second object ball; (4) cue ball strikes two cushions, then strikes first object ball, and then strikes one or more cushions before striking the second object ball.

3. Three cushions means three impacts. The number of cushions does not mean three different ones; a valid count may be executed on one cushion, if they are the result of the overspin or underspin on the ball.

4. Lagging for the Break. (1) The two players select a cue ball, which is placed on the table within the head string, and stroke the ball to the foot of the table and return. The side rails may be touched by the ball in lagging, though it is not required. (2) Player whose ball comes to rest nearest to the head rail wins the lag. (3) The winner of the lag has the right to shoot the first shot or assign the break shot to the opponent. (4) Winner of the lag has the choice of cue balls, which is then used for the duration of the game.

5. Break Shot. (1) Opponent's ball is placed on the head spot. Starting player's cue ball is placed within eight inches to the right or left of the head spot. Red ball is placed on the foot spot. (2) Starting player must contact red ball first. Failure to contact red ball first is an error and ends the starting player's inning.

(3) On subsequent shots, either red ball or cue ball can be the first object ball.

6. Fouls Which End a Player's Turn. (1) Jumped balls (Rule 11). (2) Starting play while balls are in motion. (3) Touching any of the balls by hand, part of clothing, cue or any other object such as chalk or pen. The balls shall remain in position to which they were thus moved. (4) Push or shove shot (Rule 15). (5) Double stroke (Rule 15). (6) When, at moment of shooting, neither foot is touching the floor. (7) Wrong ball (Rule 8). (8) Touching ball with cue during warm-up (Rule 18). (9) Player interference (Rule 20).

7. Any foul caused by outside interference is not to be charged as a penalty to the player with shot in progress. If the balls are displaced by the disturbance, they will be restored to their original position as precisely as possible, and the player will continue shooting.

8. Wrong Ball. (1) Shooting with the wrong ball is a foul and ends the player's inning. (2) The opponent or the referee may call this foul; opponent may call before or after the shot, while referee calls it only after the shot. (3) Such a foul can be called at any time during a run, but the shooter shall be entitled to all points made previous to the stroke in which error was detected. (4) The incoming shooter shall play the balls as left after error was called.

9. Frozen Balls. (1) If during the course of an inning the shooter's ball comes to rest in contact with the opponent's ball, the shooter has the option of playing away from the ball with which he is in contact, or elect to have the balls in contact spotted. (2) If an inning ends with the shooter's ball in contact with the next shooter's ball, or the red ball in contact with the next shooter's ball, the incoming player has the option of playing away from the ball in contact, or may elect to have the two balls which are in contact spotted. (3) Only those balls which are in contact are to be spotted. The loose or unfrozen ball is not to be touched. The red ball is spotted on the foot spot, the player's cue ball on the head spot, and the opponent's cue ball on the center spot. (4) If the spot reserved for the ball to be spotted is hidden by another ball, the ball to be spotted is placed on the spot usually reserved for the hiding ball. (5) The same rules apply when a ball or balls jump the table.

10. When a cue ball is frozen to a cushion, a player may shoot into (play against) that cushion, but the first contact shall not count. Subsequent contacts with the same cushion are valid.

11. When a player's cue ball, the opponent's ball, or the red ball jumps the table, it is a foul and the player's inning ends. Spot balls by Rule 9 (3,4).

12. No shot can be started while balls are still in motion, or are still spinning. If a player disregards this rule, it is a foul and inning ends.

13. When the cue ball bounces and rides the top of the rail and returns to the table, the ball is in play. It shall count as one cushion. If it rides two or more rails, each rail will count as a cushion. If ball remains on top of the rail, it is considered a jumped ball, which is a foul, and player's inning ends.

14. If in playing a shot the cue ball leaves the playing surface and rides the rail or cushion, regardless of the number of impacts on that cushion, only one impact will be allowed.

15. If a player has pushed or shoved the cue ball with his cue, it is a foul and player's inning ends. A push shot is one in which the cue tip remains in contact with the cue ball after cue ball strikes an object ball, or when cue tip again contacts the cue ball after cue ball strikes the object ball. Double stroke is similar and occurs when player's tip or cue shaft hits cue ball twice. If a billiard is made, it shall not count, and the player's inning ends.

16. All kiss shots are fair, whether they deprive a player of an imminent score, or whether they assist in a score.

17. Miscues shall not end the player's inning, unless it is construed that the player's ferrule or shaft also touched the cue ball. Not all miscues are fouls, and if a billiard is completed in the miscue stroke, it shall be counted and turn continues.

18. If a player during the "warm-up" stroking should touch the cue ball, it is a foul and inning ends.

19. A game is official when a player scores the number of points designated as constituting a game, even though the opponent has had one less turn at the table. If a scorekeeper is used, the game becomes official after the score sheet is signed by the players. The referee and the scorekeeper should also sign the sheet. After the losing player signs the score sheet, no protest can be made.

20. If a player at the table is responsible for interference in any manner, it is a foul, and the inning ends. Incoming player must accept balls in position. A player not at the table must not distract the opponent with undue motions or noise. The referee or tournament official may issue a warning or disqualify the player for unsportsmanlike conduct.

21. If, for reasons beyond his control, a player cannot start a game as scheduled, the game may be postponed if the tournament director so decides. If a player is unable to finish a game, he forfeits the game, unless the opponent waives the forfeiture and agrees to finish the game at a time convenient to the tournament management. If a player is unable to return to the tournament, all his games are nullified as they would be in disqualification.

2. If a player is disqualified in a game, he loses that game and gets no points. The opponent is credited with a game won and is given the number of points he would have scored had he won the game. If a player is disqualified from a tournament, all his games are nullified (that is, games played and games remaining on the schedule). Tournament continues as though one less player started when tournament opened.

23. If, for reasons beyond his control, a player cannot start a game, he must notify the tournament manager in time to allow for a substitute player, or for another pair of players. All tournament contestants are subject to immediate call if a substitute is necessary.

24. If a referee is officiating and considers a player to be taking an abnormal amount of time between strokes or in determining the choice of shots with the intention of upsetting his opponent, the referee shall warn the player that he runs the risk of disqualification if he pursues these tactics. Continued disregard of the

warning shall be proper grounds to disqualify the player. If no referee is officiating, the tournament manager shall have the right to invoke this rule.

25. Deliberate safeties are not allowed. If played, the incoming player may accept balls as they are, or set up a break shot.

26. At any tournament sanctioned by the USBA, the tournament director plus some other member of the USBA who is not playing in the tournament shall constitute a grievance committee to whom unsportsmanlike conduct during the tournament may be reported. Before commencement of the tournament, the players shall designate two of the players to serve on such a committee to protect the interests of the players. The two persons representing the USBA and the two persons representing the players shall jointly consider any evidence or reports of unsportsmanlike conduct. If this grievance committee is unable to resolve the complaint, the representatives shall submit a written report to the USBA for consideration by the Board of Directors. The two player representatives may indicate their concurrence in the findings of the USBA representatives or may submit dissenting views to the Board of Directors. At the next regular meeting or special meeting of the Board of Directors, these reports shall be considered and the action recommended by a majority shall be binding on the accused member of the USBA.

THE DIAMOND SYSTEM

There are various systems in billiards which make use of the spots, or diamonds, inset in the rails. Numerical values assigned to the diamonds enable players to plan shots, particularly banks shots, with the help of simple arithmetic. Some world-class players don't use diamond systems, some use them only to check their instint or judgment, and some use them at every opportunity. The fact is, on many shots in three-cushion billiards, diamond systems greatly reduce the need for guesswork. What follows is a description of the most widely-used system, the "corner 5," also called "the diamond system," or simply "the system."

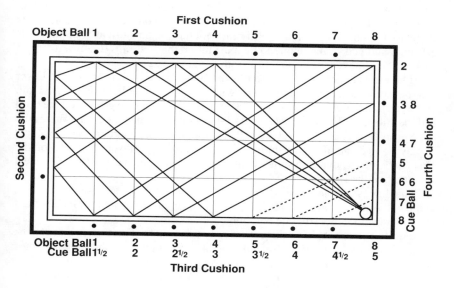

A cue ball hit with slight running english that strikes the third rail at diamond No. 1 will travel back to diamond No. 7 on the first cushion. If it strikes diamond No. 2 on the third rail it will travel back to diamond No. 8 on the first rail (or corner). Diamond No. 3 on the third rail connects with diamond No. 3 (object ball number) on the lower rail. The various diamonds connect as illustrated in the diagram. A player must memorize these connections to use the diamond system, since he must know the path the ball will travel after it comes off the third rail.

Playing the diamond system the player studies his shot backwards–that is, he must find out where he will come off the third cushion to score. Say, for example, that both object balls lie in the upper right corner of the diagram, with the cue ball in the lower right corner as shown.

The player, having memorized the connecting diamonds, knows that he must come off diamond No. 2 on the third rail to bank the shot in that corner.

Note that there are object ball markings on the third cushion. They start from No. 1 at the first diamond and go up to 8 which is the corner. If the player has to come off the second diamond, his object ball number is 2.

Note there are cue ball numbers on the third cushion. They start with 1-$\frac{1}{2}$ on the first diamond and go up to 5, which is the corner. The cue ball numbers also continue on the lower rail, as 6, 7, and 8. (See diagram.)

The player is still playing the bank shot with the two object balls in the upper right hand corner. He knows up to this time that he must come off diamond No. 2 on the third rail to count.

He must figure out where he will hit on the first cushion to bring his cue ball back to diamond No. 2 on the third cushion. In the diagram the cue ball lies at cue ball No. 5, which is the corner. Thus, knowing the object ball number (2) and the cue ball number (5), he subtracts the object ball number (2) from the cue ball number (5) and gets 3, which is the diamond he must hit on the first rail. If he wants to get to diamond No. 1 on the third rail, with the cue ball still at 5, he subtracts 1 from 5 and gets 4, the diamond he must hit on the first rail. If he wants to get to 3 on the third rail, he subtracts 3 from 5 and gets 2.

If he wants to get 2 on the third rail and finds the cue ball is at 6 on the lower rail, he subtracts 2 from 6 and gets 4 which is where he will hit on the first rail. If the cue ball lies at 3-$\frac{1}{2}$ as a cue ball number and he wants to get to 2 on the third rail, he subtracts 2 from 3-$\frac{1}{2}$ and gets 1-$\frac{1}{2}$, which he must hit on the first rail.

Note that when a ball lies at cue ball position No. 5 (see diagram) and the player is playing to come off the cushion at 2 on the third rail, player must hit 3 on the first cushion. The diagram shows a line running from cue ball position 5 to the 3 diamond on the first cushion.

That line is cue ball position 5, no matter where the cue ball rests on that line. If the ball is in the corner it is 5. If the cue ball is on the line and four inches from the first cushion, it is still cue ball number 5.

Our discussion to this point covers only bank shots. The system can also be used when a ball is hit first. Consider the position in the second diagram (next page). In shots of this type, the first object ball gives the player his cue ball number. Suppose the first object ball lies on the line of cue ball position 5 we discussed immediately above. If the player drove the object ball on cue ball line 5 into the first cushion at diamond No. 3, he would hit the third cushion at 2 and travel to the lower right hand corner; assuming the second object ball is in that corner.

However, the player cannot drive the object ball with his cue. So–knowing the first object ball rests on cue ball line 5, he must drive the cue ball from the first object ball into the first cushion at diamond No. 3 to come off the third rail at diamond No. 2 and make the shot on the second object ball in the lower right hand corner. Here, the ability to make caroms reveals its importance.

The most important thing in 3-cushion billiards is being able to drive the cue ball from the first object ball into the first cushion at the point desired. In other words, unless the player can make the simple carom of driving the cue ball from the first object ball into the desired point of the first cushion, his chances of making the count are minimized.

If the first object ball lies on cue ball track (or line) 4-$\frac{1}{2}$ and the player wants to come off diamond No. 2 on the third cushion, he subtracts 2 from 4-$\frac{1}{2}$ and then proceeds to drive his cue ball off the first object ball into 2-$\frac{1}{2}$ on the first cushion (which is 2 from 4-$\frac{1}{2}$).

Many players refuse to learn the diamond system, because written explanations of it are somewhat complicated and require studious attention. However, if the player will follow the instructions above and test them out on a table, he will find the system is comparatively simple. Oral explanations from a player who knows the system make for easier understanding, of course.

The diamond system is not infallible, but on bank shots particularly it serves a player better than his instinct. If you watch a player in world's tournaments as he studies a bank shot, he will determine first from what point he must come off the third rail to score.

Say he has to come off diamond 2-$\frac{1}{2}$ on the third rail. He then determines his cue ball number. Say it is 4-$\frac{1}{2}$. By subtracting 2-$\frac{1}{2}$ from 4-$\frac{1}{2}$ he knows he must hit diamond No. 2 on the first rail to get back to diamond No. 2-$\frac{1}{2}$ on the third rail. The system tells him exactly where to hit. His instinct may have given him the general location of the desired point on the first cushion, but if he hit 1-$\frac{3}{4}$ or 2-$\frac{1}{4}$ on the first rail, chances are he would miss the shot.

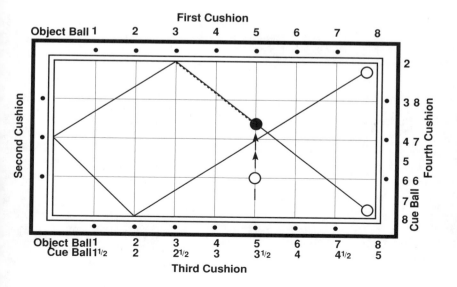

When using the diamond system, strike the cue ball above center with running english, following through on your stroke. If you stab the cue ball with a jerky stroke you will shorten the angle. If you slam the cue ball too hard you are likely to shorten the angle. Use a stroke of medium force and follow through.

If the balls do not lie exactly on the object ball and cue ball tracks, you may parallel or you may figure the diamonds in fractions. For example, if the object ball number is 1-$\frac{1}{4}$ and the cue ball number is 3-$\frac{1}{2}$, your subtraction gives you point 2-$\frac{1}{4}$ on the first rail. The diamond system does not apply to all shots on the table. It is confined almost entirely to natural angle shots.

You may find that in using the diamond system on a certain table that your cue ball "comes short." If this happens, you allow for it in your calculations, moving up higher on the first rail. Thus, instead of hitting 2 (assuming your calculations tell you to hit 2) you move down to 1-$\frac{3}{4}$ or maybe 1-$\frac{1}{2}$. Make sure first, however, that you are stroking your cue ball with running english and are following through before you decide the table runs "short."

When using the diamond system, aim at the diamond through the cushion—that is, at an angle through the cushion to the diamond, which is set back on the rail. Do not aim at a point at the edge of the cushion which is directly opposite the diamond.

THREE-CUSHION PRACTICE SHOTS

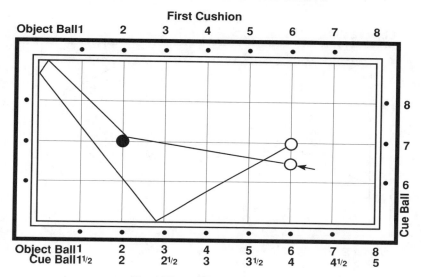

First Cushion

Object Ball	1	2	3	4	5	6	7	8

	1	2	3	4	5	6	7	8
Object Ball	1	2	3	4	5	6	7	8
Cue Ball	1½	2	2½	3	3½	4	4½	5

No. 1 Three Cushion Shot

Hold cue level. Hit object ball 1/3 right. Strike cue ball center, slight english left. Use 7 inch bridge. Use moderate stroke.

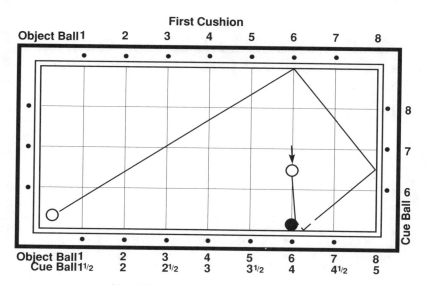

First Cushion

Object Ball	1	2	3	4	5	6	7	8

	1	2	3	4	5	6	7	8
Object Ball	1	2	3	4	5	6	7	8
Cue Ball	1½	2	2½	3	3½	4	4½	5

No. 2 Three or Four Cushion Shot

Hold cue level. Hit object ball 1/4 left. Strike cue ball center, english left. Use 6 inch bridge. Use moderate stroke.

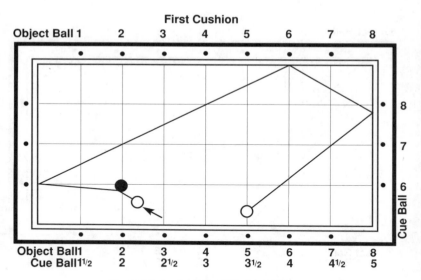

No. 3 Three or Four Cushion Shot

Hold cue level. Hit object ball 1/4 left. Strike cue ball center, english right. Use 7 inch bridge. Use moderate stroke.

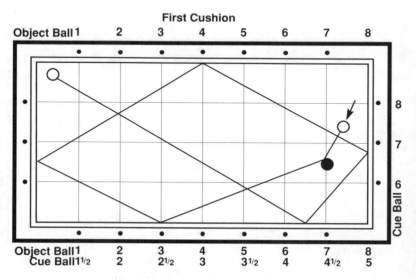

No. 4 Five or Six Cushion Shot

Hold cue level. Hit object ball thin. Strike cue ball center, english right. Use 8 inch bridge. Use hard stroke.

BCA HALL OF FAME

The purpose of the Hall of Fame is to honor outstanding persons of the world who, through their competitive skills and dedication, have enriched the game of billiards.

Two categories have been established in BCA's Hall of Fame. The **Greatest Players** category shall be reserved for outstanding players who have reached 40 years of age within the calendar year it is awarded and who have been active in national or foreign competition for at least 20 years and have won at least one national or foreign championship recognized by the BCA. At least one candidate from this category will be nominated annually. The **Meritorious Service** category shall be reserved for persons who have made lasting, memorable and important contributions to billiards, even though they may not have distinguished themselves as competitors.

Pictured on the following pages are those who have the distinct honor of membership in the BCA Hall of Fame.

Ralph Greenleaf
1899-1950
inducted 1966

Fourteen-time World Pocket Billiard Champion, RALPH GREENLEAF, possessed all the flash and flair of a natural showman. With his beautiful actress wife, Princess Nai Tai Tai, the handsome Greenleaf put together a sparkling trick-shot performance and toured the vaudeville circuit in the 20s and 30s. The audiences watched him perform his spectacular shots by looking at a huge mirror suspended on stage over the playing table.

Greenleaf won his first Pocket Billiard championship in 1919 and his last one in 1937.

William F. Hoppe
1887-1959
inducted 1966

WILLIE HOPPE, whose brilliant career was one of the longest in the annals of the sport, is considered by many to be the greatest all-around billiard player of any era.

In 1906, at the tender age of 18, Hoppe won his first world's title by defeating the renowned French champion, Maurice Vignaux, at 18.1 Balkline in a memorable match in Paris. He went on to win the 18.2 Balkline and Cushion Carom titles and years later, between 1936 and 1952, held the Three-Cushion title 11 times.

Charles C. Peterson
1880-1962
inducted 1966

CHARLIE PETERSON earned the title "Missionary of Billiards" for his untiring efforts to promote the game throughout the United States.

In addition to being the world's fancy-shot champion and, for years, holder of the Red Ball title, Peterson made scores of personal appearances at colleges and universities across the country and was the guiding spirit of the Intercollegiate and Boys' Clubs of America tournaments.

Peterson died at the age of 83, after a life devoted to winning friends for the sport of billiards.

Welker Cochran
1896-1959
inducted 1967

WELKER COCHRAN, a champion who trained for his billiard matches with the same intensity as a professional boxer, won his first of two 18.2 Balkline titles in 1927. He later went on to become the Three-Cushion champion five times in the 30s and 40s.

Like many stars of the sport, Cochran learned the game in his father's billiard establishment, and he became the protege of Frank Gotch, the wrestler, who sent young Cochran to Chicago to hone his playing talents.

Alfredo DeOro
1862-1948
inducted 1967

The career of the distinguished Spanish champion, ALFREDO DeORO, encompassed both Three-Cushion and Pocket Billiards and spanned the closing decades of the 19th century and the opening decades of the 20th.

DeOro, who served in his country's diplomatic corps, first gained the Pocket Billiard crown in 1887. He was to repeat the achievement 16 times in the next 25 years. DeOro held the Three-Cushion title 10 times from 1908 through 1919.

In 1934, at the age of 71, DeOro came out of retirement for a Championship Tournament, winning two dramatic victories from defending champion Welker Cochran and the ultimate winner of the tournament, Johnny Layton.

Benjamin B. Nartzik
1895-1963
inducted 1967

BEN NARTZIK will always be remembered for his tireless crusade to revive billiards from its severe doldrums in the 1950s. Nartzik deserves a lion's share of the credit for ridding the game of its "pool hall" image and re-establishing its status as a "gentleman's sport." Under his leadership, the BCA was able to help both the Boys Club of America and the Association of College Unions to organize billiard programs and run successful annual tournaments. Nartzik recognized the potential of the industry and bought the National Billiard Chalk Co. of Chicago.

Willie Mosconi
1913-Present
inducted 1968

For most people, the name WILLIE MOSCONI and the sport of Pocket Billiards are synonymous. And rightly so, since from 1940 to 1957 Mosconi had a near-stranglehold on the World Title, winning it 15 times in that period. Born in Philadelphia in 1913, Willie was a prodigy with the cue by the age of seven. At 20, he embarked on a hectic cross-country exhibition tour with his idol, Ralph Greenleaf, then World Champ and at the height of his game. The result, 57 wins for Greenleaf, an amazing 50 wins for the young Mosconi. One of the most astounding of Mosconi's many records is his yet-unbroken exhibition high run of 526 balls!

Jake Schaefer, Sr.
1855-1910
inducted 1968

"A player whose super-brilliance with a billiard cue won for him the sobriquet of 'Wizard'..." so runs the lead of a 1909 newspaper article singing the praises of JAKE SCHAEFER, SR. From the last quarter of the 19th century through the first decade of the 20th, Schaefer, Sr. was one of the most feared names in Balkline Billiards. Derivations of the game were invented just to stymie his genius – all unsuccessfully. He traveled throughout the world winning matches and gathering fans. On March 11, 1908, though desperately ill, he success-fully defended his title in his final match for the 18.1 championship against Willie Hoppe by a score of 500 to 423.

Jake Schaefer, Jr.
1894-1975
inducted 1968

Billiard historians generally rank JAKE SCHAEFER, JR. as the greatest of the American Balkline players. He was the world champion at 18.2 in 1921, 1925, 1926, 1927, and 1929-1933. He held the 18.1 honors in 1926-1927 and the 28.2 title in 1937-1938. At the 18.2 game, he holds four records which have never been equalled in this country: best game average, 400 (from the break); grand average, tournament, 57.14; grand average, match, 93.25; high run, match, 432.

Herman J. Rambow
1881-1967
inducted 1969

Called the Stradivari of his trade by those who know, HER-MAN RAMBOW crafted custom cues for the greatest players in billiards over the course of a 65-year career. Captains of industry and celebrities of the entertainment world also beat a path to his door to have the privilege of paying from $50 to $300 for one of his perfectly-balanced "Rambow Specials." It was Herman who perfected the jointed cue by inserting a countersunk screw in the recessed butt end, making an extra-sturdy connection. Only death at age 86 stopped the craftsman from his labor of love. To billiard cognoscenti the world over, there will never be another Rambow.

Harold Worst
1929-1966
inducted 1970

HAROLD WORST of Grand Rapids, Michigan was only 19 years old when he played the great Willie Hoppe, winner of 51 major billiard championships, in a demonstration game in Detroit in 1949. Hoppe soon took an interest in Worst's playing potential, and under his guidance, Worst won the world title for three-cushion billiards in Argentina in 1954, the youngest player to compete in world competition. He successfully defended this title for many years. Equally skilled at pocket billiards, Worst dominated play to win the All-Around titles in both the 1965 Johnston City, IL and 1965 Stardust Open championships.

John Wesley Hyatt
1837-1920
inducted 1971

JOHN WESLEY HYATT, known as the father of the American plastic industry, was an inventor rather than a player, but his invention of the celluloid plastic billiard ball in 1868 revolutionized the billiard industry. Hyatt began his search for a suitable synthetic billiard ball material when a New York billiards firm offered a $10,000 prize for a substitute for ivory. Hyatt's earlier attempts involved shellacking a paper pulp sphere and a ball made of layers of cloth.

Frank Taberski
1889-1941
inducted 1975

FRANK TABERSKI grew up in Schenectady, N.Y. At the age of 26, he attended a pocket billiard championship in New York City, and came home convinced he played as well as the champions. The next year, he entered and placed third behind Johnny Layton. From then on, he was almost invincible. In those days, 450 point challenge matches were the means of competition; the prize a ruby and diamond studded gold medal with the proviso that any one who won 10 consecutive challenge matches could keep it. Alfredo DeOro had come closest with five straight defenses. By 1918 Taberski had accomplished the impossible and the medal was his.

Johnny Layton
1887-1956
inducted 1976

JOHNNY LAYTON, born in Sedalia, Mo., won the world's three-cushion championship 12 times, defeating such champions as Willie Hoppe, Welker Cochran, Jake Schaefer, Jr. and Augie Kieckhefer in the 1920s and 1930s. Layton recorded the high three-cushion game mark of 50 points in 23 innings, a record which still stands today. He was credited with originating the method of using the diamond system, using table markers to indicate direction of ball rebounds, a style that he perfected through the application of his highly developed mathematical mind.

James Caras
1910-Present
inducted 1977

JIMMY CARAS was born in Scranton, Pennsylvania, and is the second living person to be elected to the Hall of Fame. Jimmy started playing billiards at the age of five. When 17, he defeated Ralph Greenleaf in an exhibition match to become known as the Boy Wonder of The World . Nine years later, in 1936, he won his first world championship. He won again in 1938, 1939 and in 1949. Eighteen years later, in 1967, he won the U.S. Open in a field of 48 players. His record of "most balls," "most games won" and "fewest innings by a champion" still stand in the record book for that size field.

Irving Crane
1913-Present
inducted 1978

IRVING CRANE was born in Livonia, New York. His love for the game started as a child, when he was given a toy billiard table. Although he played steadily as a teenager, he did not enter tournament play until the age of 23. He won his first world title in 1942. Since then, he has won almost two dozen major championships, including the world crown in 1946, 1955, 1966, 1968, 1970, 1972, plus the International Roundrobin championship in 1968.

Crane was the victor in the 1978 World Series of Billiards (a combination of 14.1 and 9-ball) against a strong field of outstanding competitors. His greatest triumph, however, was his victory in the 1966 U.S. Open, when he won the championship in a never-to-be-excelled record run of 150 and out.

Steve Mizerak
1944-Present
inducted 1980

STEVE MIZERAK, born in Perth Amboy, New Jersey, was the youngest inductee to the BCA Hall of Fame. In the brief span of his career, he has been 4 times champion of the U.S. Open, winning the title in 1970, 1971, 1972, and 1973. Mizerak also captured the PPPA World Open title in 1982 and 1983. Mizerak continues to finish near the top in several national tournaments each year.

Dorothy Wise
1914-Present
inducted 1981

DOROTHY WISE was born in Spokane, Washington. In her early years, there were very few national tournaments for women. Since she was in many local and state tournaments, she became the self-proclaimed world champion. When BCA staged the first national tournament for women in 1967, she immediately entered. For the next five years, she proved herself most worthy as she won five consecutive U.S. Open titles.

Joseph Balsis
1921-Present
inducted 1982

JOE BALSIS was born in Minnersville, Pa. Balsis never could resist knocking the balls around one of the pool tables at father John Balsis' recreation room. By the time he was 11, Balsis was playing exhibitions against the likes of Andrew Ponzi and Erwin Rudolph. He won junior titles four consecutive years. During pool's doldrum years Balsis left the game and it wasn't until 1944 that Balsis, a boat machinist in the Coast Guard, won his next title; Armed Services Champ. In 1964 "the Meatman," as Balsis is known because of his family's meat business, returned to competitive pool. Between 1965 and 1975 Balsis competed in the finals of the U.S. Open five times, winning twice (1968 & 1974). He won the prestigious Billiard Room Proprietor's Association tournament in 1965, then captured the World All-Around championship in Johnston City, Ill., in 1966. He won the Jansco brothers' Stardust Open all-around title back-to-back in 1968 and 1969.

Luther Lassiter
1919-1988
inducted 1983

Considered by many to be the finest 9-ball player ever, LUTHER LASSITER was born in Elizabeth City, NC. Lassiter earned his nickname "Wimpy," for all the hot dogs and Orange Crushes he could pack away as a youngster hanging around the local pool hall. By the time he was seventeen, "Wimpy" was packing away his share of opponents. Lassiter's biggest years in tournament play came in the 1960s. In the eleven years of the Jansco brothers' all-around championships in Johnston City, IL (1962-1972), Lassiter won the straight pool title five times, the nine-ball title four times and the one-pocket title once. On three occasions Lassiter went on to capture the All-Around title (1962, 1963, 1967). He also won the BCA U.S. Open in 1967 and the Stardust World All-Around championship in 1971.

"Minnesota Fats"
1913-Present
inducted 1984

Perhaps the most recognizable figure in the history of pool, RUDOLPH "Minnesota Fats" WANDERONE was elected to the Hall of Fame for Meritorious Service. Although he never actually won a designated "world championship" Wanderone, the game's leading comic, orator and publicity generator, has probably done more for the game in terms of sheer exposure than any other player. Initially nicknamed "Brooklyn Fats," and "New York Fats," Wanderone dubbed himself "Minnesota Fats" after the film version of "The Hustler" hit movie screens around the country in the early 1960's. Since that time he has become known around the world as pool's foremost side show. "Fats," whose exact age is a mystery, hosted a national television show, "Celebrity Billiards," during the 1960s. He stopped playing in tournaments all together around that time.

Jean Balukas
1959-Present
inducted 1985

JEAN BALUKAS is the second woman inducted into the BCA Hall of Fame. She was born in Brooklyn, New York, and is the Hall's youngest member. An excellent all-around athlete, Jean competed in her first BCA U.S. Open when she was nine years old, finishing seventh. She won her first BCA crown when she was 12. Since then Jean has collected seven BCA U.S. Open 14.1 titles, six World Open titles and countless 9-ball and straight pool crowns. She has been named Player of the Year five times.

Lou Butera
1938-Present
inducted 1986

LOU BUTERA was born in Pittston, Pennsylvania. He learned to play at his father's pool room in the small coal-mining town. After watching BCA Hall of Famer Erwin Rudolph in an exhibition, 14-year-old Lou decided to devote his life to pool. He was runner-up to Irving Crane in the 1972 World Championship in Los Angeles. In 1973 he defeated Crane in the finals of the same event to win his first World Championship. Nicknamed "Machine Gun Lou" for his rapid fire style, Lou recorded a 150-ball run against Allen Hopkins in just 21 minutes in 1973. Butera has since won numerous titles.

Erwin Rudolph
1894-1957
inducted 1987

ERWIN RUDOLPH was born in Cleveland. Rudolph did not participate in his first world 14.1 championship until he was 24 years old. Five years later, in 1926, Rudolph gained national acclaim by ending Ralph Greenleaf's six-year reign as world champion. Rudolph's win over Greenleaf came in a challenge match. After losing his world title to Thomas Hueston, Rudolph regained the crown by winning the 1933 world championship. He won his third world title in 1933, and, at age 47, captured his fourth and final world crown by defeating a young Irving Crane in the finals of the 1941 world championship in Philadelphia. At the time of his death in 1957, he held the record for fastest game in a world tournament, scoring 125 points in just 32 minutes. (The record has since been eclipsed.)

Andrew Ponzi
1903-1950
inducted 1988

ANDREW PONZI was born Andrew D'Allesandro in Phila-delphia. He acquired the name Ponzi after a witness to his cue prowess compared the likelihood of beating D'Allesandro with beating the infamous "Ponzi Scheme," an early version of the pyramid game. A dazzling offensive player, Ponzi com-peted in the game's Golden Era, the 1930s and 1940s, against the likes of Mosconi, Crane, Caras, Rudolph and Greenleaf. Despite that stiff competition, Ponzi captured World 14.1 titles in 1934, 1940 and 1943.

Michael Sigel
1953-Present
inducted 1989

MIKE SIGEL, at 35, became the youngest male elected to the BCA Hall of Fame. Born in Rochester, N.Y. Sigel began playing pool at 13, and turned professional when he was 20. A natural right-hander who shoots left-handed, Sigel won his first major tournament, the U.S. Open 9-Ball Championship, in 1975. His career blossomed quickly, and Sigel was perhaps the game's dominant player in the 1980s. He amassed 38 major 14.1 and 9-ball championships in that decade. Sigel has won three World 14.1 crowns (1979, 1981 and 1985) and one World 9-Ball title (1985) as well as numerous national titles.

John Brunswick
1819-1886
inducted 1990

JOHN BRUNSWICK was a Swiss immigrant woodworker who founded what has become the Brunswick Corporation, the largest pool table manufacturer in this country. Producing his first billiard table in 1845, Brunswick went on to develop an American market for billiard equipment. He is credited with the rapid growth of billiards in the late 19th century.

Walter Tevis
1928-1984
inducted 1991

WALTER TEVIS is best remembered as the author of two popular novels about pool, *The Hustler* and *The Color of Money*. Both books were made into enormously successful movies starring Paul Newman. *The Hustler* documented pool culture in the United States in the late 1950s and *The Color of Money* followed up on the same theme twenty-five years later. Both movies were directly responsible for igniting strong uptrends in pocket billiards during the years immediately following their releases. Tevis wrote numerous short stories and several other novels including *The Man Who Fell To Earth* (a sciencefiction thriller) and *The Queen's Gambit* (a portrait of a female chess master). He was a Milton scholar and held two masters degrees (from the University of Kentucky and the Writers' Workshop at the University of Iowa). He taught creative writing at Ohio University from 1965 to 1978. His works have been translated into many languages and are popular all over the world

Nick Varner
1948-Present
inducted 1992

Learning the basics of pool at an early age from his father in his hometown of Owensboro, Kentucky, NICK VARNER displayed his great overall talents in 14.1, Nine Ball, One Pocket and Bank Pool by claiming the 1969 and 1970 national ACU-I collegiate titles, the World 14.1 Championship in 1980 amd 1986 and the BCA National Eight Ball Championship in 1980. Accumulating over 20 major titles in his career, he became only the second man to earn over $100,000 in prize winnings in the memorable 1989 season in which he won eight of the sixteen major Nine Ball events. Winner of the Player of the Year in 1980 and 1989, and the first honoree of the MPBA Sportsperson of the Year in 1991, Nick has always been an exemplary role model and has enriched the sport of pocket billiards through his many years of dedication to excellence and sportsmanship.

TOURNAMENT RESULTS
AND RECORDS

For records of tournaments no longer held, check the listings at the back of this section first and then prior editions of the BCA Official Rules and Record Book.

BCA NATIONAL EIGHT BALL INDIVIDUAL CHAMPIONS
Open Men's Division

1977–Tom Kilburn, South Bend, IN, ...Runner-up–Dick Spitzer
1978–Mike Carella, Louisville, KY, ...Runner-up–Bob Williams
1979–Jimmy Reid, Louisvile, KY, ...Runner-up–Mark Wilson
1980–Nick Varner, Owensboro, KY, ...Runner-up–Mike Massey
1981–Danny Diliberto, Buffalo, NY, ...Runner-up–Nick Varner
1982–Joe Sposit, Pittshara, MO, ...Runner-up–Gregg Fix
1983–Michael Sardelli, Detroit, MI, ...Runner-up–Tom Chapman
1984–Louie Lemke, Fort Worth, TX, ...Runner-up–Charles Shootman
1985–Steve Matlock, Cedar Rapids, IA, ...Runner-up–Stan Fimple
1986–Jesus Rivera, CO, ...Runner-up–Mickey Leon Stone
1987–Stan Fimple, Omaha, NE, ...Runner-up–Mike Fenne
1988–Harry Sexton, Detroit, MI, ...Runner-up–Seco Varani
1989–Henry Granas, Englewood, CO, ...Runner-up–T.J. Davis
1990–Jesus Rivera, Denver, CO, ...Runner-up–Gilbert Martinez
1991–Paul Guernsey, Plano,TX, ...Runner-up–Gene Rossi
1992–Allan Jones, Porter, IN, ...Runner-up–James Hevener

Master Men's Division

1992–David Gutierrez, Houston, TX, ...Runner-up–Marv Rapp

Open Women's Division

1978–Catherine Stephens, Louisville, KY, ...Runner-up–Melodie Horn
1979–Gloria Walker, Louisville, KY, ...Runner-up–Mary Kenniston
1980–Billie Billing, Columbus, OH, ...Runner-up–Gloria Walker
1981–Belinda Campos, Las Vegas, NV, ...Runner-up–Sherry Lively
1982–Linda Hoffman, Kansas City, MO, ...Runner-up–Sherry Lively
1983–Georgina Casteel, Detroit, MI, ...Runner-up–Sherry Lively
1984–Belinda Campos Bearden, Fort Worth, TX, ... Runner-up–Linda Hoffman
1985–Linda Hoffman, Arlington, TX, ...Runner-up–Diane Piercy
1986–Linda Hoffman, Arlington, TX, ...Runner-up–Christine Glass
1987–Linda Hoffman, Arlington, TX, ...Runner-up–Janene Hague
1988–Timi Bloomberg, Rapid City, SD, ...Runner-up–Kathy Miao
1989–Sherry Lively, Carmichael, CA, ...Runner-up–Christine Glass
1990–Linda Meyer, Ponca City, OK, ...Runner-up–Janene Hague
1991–Suzi Quall, Appleton,WI, ...Runner-up–Chris Fields
1992–Brenda Plantz, Louisville, CO, ...Runner-up–Cindy Doty

Master Women's Division

1992–Linda Stepanski, Milwaukee, WI, ...Runner-up–Ellen Sellers

Senior Men's Division

1986–Stanley Coscia, Tampa, FL, ...Runner-up–Harold Schnormeier
1987–Jerry Priest, Cape Girardeau, MO, ...Runner-up–Bob Keating

1988–Seco Varani, Faribault, MN, ...Runner-up–Bob Keating
1989–Jerry Priest, Cape Girardeau, MO, ...Runner-up–Bob Vanover
1990–Jerry Priest, Cape Girardeau, MO, ...Runner-up–Bernard Rogoff
1991–Bob Vanover, Dallas,TX, ...Runner-up–Beau Zimmerman
1992–Seco Varani, Faribault, MN, ...Runner-up–Fred Guarino

Senior Women's Division

1989–Fern Reedy, Smithville, MO, ...Runner-up–Jeanne Bloomberg
1990–Jeri Engh, Osceola, WI, ...Runner-up–Op Wheeler
1991–Karen Wold, St. Paul,MN,..Runner-up–Lynn Reed
1992–Lynn Reed, New Berlin, WI, ...Runner-up–Charlene Edwards

BCA NATIONAL EIGHT BALL
SCOTCH-DOUBLES CHAMPIONS

1991 ....Bonnie and Mark Coats (Broken Arrow, OK)
1992 ....Maureen Finn/Pete Lewis (Clinton, IA)

BCA NATIONAL EIGHT BALL TEAM CHAMPIONS
Master Men

1991 ....Black Sticks (Houston, TX)
1992 ....The Crunch Bunch (Dallas, TX)

Women

1979 .... Wheel Inn (Billings, MT)
1980 .... Burt's Girls (Colorado Springs, CO)
1981 .... Burt's Girls (Colorado Springs, CO)
1982 .... Richard's (Lansing, MI)
1983 .... Richard's (Lansing, MI)
1984 .... North Star (Sacramento, CA)
1985 .... Gold Nugget (Arlington, TX)
1986 .... Leisure Club (Phoenix, AZ)
1987 .... Leftys + (Sacramento, CA)
1988 . Great American Girls (Sacramento, CA)
1989 .... 8-Ball Express (Rapid City, SD)
1990 .... 8-Ball Express (Rapid City, SD)
1991 .... Cue-T s (West Allis, WI)
1992 .... Lucky Ladies (Ft. Worth, TX)

Men

1979 . Tam O'Shanter (Colorado Springs, CO)
1980 . Tam O'Shanter (Colorado Springs, CO)
1981 . Tam O'Shanter (Colorado Springs, CO)
1982 ...... The Wizards (Colorado Springs, CO)
1983 .... Mike's Lounge (Pittsburgh, PA)
1984 .... Green Acres (Ft. Worth, TX)
1985 .... Starlite Lounge (Arlington, TX)
1986 .... MeMaws (Ft. Worth, TX)
1987 ..... Jackson All Stars (Grand Prairie, TX)
1988 ... Mongo Murph's (Windsor, CANADA)
1989 .... Black Sticks (Houston, TX)
1990 .... Black Sticks (Houston, TX)
1991 .... Players (San Antonio, TX)
1992 .... Lassiters (Clinton, IA)

BCA NATIONAL JUNIOR EIGHT BALL CHAMPIONS

1989–Chan Whitt, Jr., Lewisburg, WV, ...Runner-up–Chad Duster
1990–Nathan Haddad, Lansing, MI (15-18 division) ....Runner-up–Scott Marshall
    –Michael Coltrain, Raleigh, NC (14 and under) ....Runner-up–Chris Whitten
1991–Max Eberle, Arlington, VA (15-18 division) ....Runner-up–Chan Whitt
    –Charles Williams, Newport News, VA (14 and under) ....Runner-up–Kelsey Jorgensen
1992–Mike Rinella, Abington, MA (15-18 division) ....Runner-up–Larry Nevel, Jr.
    –Andy Quinn, St. Charles, MO (14 and under) ....Runner-up–Jesse Bowman

BCA SANCTIONED TOURNAMENTS
THRILLA FOR THE GORILLA, BUFFALO, NY
1. Eddy Rosas, Jr.   2. Joe Wojciechowski   3. Tom Guindon   4. Larry Croisdale
SMOKIN STICK'S II EIGHT BALL, BUFFALO, NY
1. Jerry Howard   2. Fred Stonelli   3. Ed Rosas   4. Hector Rosas
SLAM IN THE SLAMMER EIGHT BALL, BUFFALO, NY
1. Phil Bullock 2. Renaldo Rendon 3. Tom Guindon 4. Jerry Cutman
SALUTE TO MARK TWAIN EIGHT BALL, BUFFALO, NY
1. Santo   2. Wilbur Monture   3. Kevin Cogan 4. Fred Stronelli

1991 BCA ROCKY MOUNTAIN OPEN, CHEYENNE, WY
1. Tracy Dunn   2. Dave Black   3. Mike Hoffman   4. Warren Webber

CHALK IT UP AT SKULSKI'S EIGHT BALL TOURNAMENT, BUFFALO, NY
1. Eddy Rosas   2. Joe Wojciechowski   3. Wilbur Monture   4. Norman Skulski, Jr.

SFEA "COMIN OUTTA THE COLD" EIGHT BALL WINTER TOURNEY, BLOOMINGTON, IL
1. John Shride   2. Brad Sipes   3. Kevin Jasperson   4. Howard Meyers

LA CUE BILLIARDS AND CAFE CLASSIC, MASPETH, NY
1. Rob Caradonna   2. Mark Halegua   3. John Drewes   4. Joe Farruggia

L.A. OPEN NINE BALL CHAMPIONSHIPS
(Men) 1. Earl Strickland   2. Johhny Archer / (Women) 1. Peg Ledman   2. JoAnn Mason-Parker

6th ANNUAL ALASKA STRAIGHT POOL CHAMPIONSHIP, ANCHORAGE, AK
1. Al Bryan   2. Wayne Boomer   3. Bill Stock   4. Don Wirtaman

SIX COUNTY SENIOR EIGHT BALL CHAMPIONSHIP, CAROL STREAM, IL
1. Colleen Byrnes .... (women 55-59 yr. old div.)
1. Harry Bostrom   2. Gene Olson .... (men 60-64 yr. old div.)
1. Charlotte McGraw .... (women 60-64 yr. old div.)
1. George Pierotti   2. Robert Wallace   3. Morman Martin .... (men 65-69 yr. old div.)
1. Dorothy Iski   2. Irene Kerwin .... (women 65-69 yr. old div.)
1. Leo Kozlowski   2. Paul Stinger   3. Andrew Zultner .... (men 70-74 yr. old div.)
1. Angel Salazar   2. Harold Schroeder   3. Loren Pierson .... (men 75-79 yr. old div.)
1. Anthony Ranieri .... (men 80-84 yr. old div.)

BROWN'S BCA NINE BALL OPEN, MARION, IN
1. Dee Adkins   2. Tony Lane   3. Steve McAninch   4. Tony Reams

6th ANNUAL WORLD OPEN HONOLULU CHAMPIONSHIP, ANCHORAGE, AK
1. Mark Owens   2. Mark Tullis   3. Mike Moore   4. Stan McElroy

SALUTE TO NORM SKULSKI TOURNEY, BUFFALO, NY
1. Hector Rosas   2. Eddie Rosas, Jr.   3. Eddie Rosas   4. Mark Hatch

1992 ABL FALL TEAM CHAMPIONSHIPS, DALLAS, TX
1. Bangers   2. Shakers   3. Right Angles   4. Mick's Masters

* BAILEY'S NINE-BALL OPEN, PITTSBURG, PA
* HARTFORD VETERAN'S EIGHT-BALL OPEN, HARTFORD, CT
* THE BAY AREA SPORTS AND HEALTH EXPERIENCE NINE-BALL BASH, SAN FRANCISCO, CA
* CAN-AM POOL TOURNEY, BUFFALO, NY
* NORTHWEST NINE-BALL CLASSIC, WOODINVILLE, WA
* SALUTE TO PAUL MEKEEL EIGHT-BALL TOURNEY, BUFFALO, NY
* No tournament results available.

ACU-I POCKET BILLIARD CHAMPIONS (Men)

1937	John O. Miller	University of Wisconsin
1938	J. L. Geiger	University of Florida
1939	Peter Choulas	Colgate University
1940	John O. Miller	University of Wisconsin
1941	Lloyd Green	University of Kansas
1942	Leo Bonimi	Cornell University
1943	L. Mabie	University of Florida
1944	J. Zvanya	University of Indiana
1945-46	(No Tournament)	
1947	Leff Mabie	University of Florida
1948	Jack Brown	University of Utah
1949	Leroy Kinman	Eastern Kentucky State

1950 .... Leroy Kinman .... Eastern Kentucky State
1951 .... Leroy Kinman .... Eastern Kentucky State
1952 .... Bill Simms .... University of Georgia
1953 .... John Beaudette .... Michigan State College
1954 .... John Beaudette .... Michigan State College
1955 .... Rodney Boyd .... Ohio State University
1956 .... Joseph Sapanaro .... Suffolk University
1957 .... Joseph Sapanaro .... Suffolk University
1958 .... Lloyd Courter .... State University of Iowa
1959 .... Donald Dull .... State College of Washington
1960 .... Henry Parks .... Indiana University
1961 .... Jim Finucane .... University of Notre Dame
1962 .... Robert Burke .... University of Oregon
1963 .... Larry Galloway .... Indiana University
1964 .... William Hendricks .... Southern Illinois University
1965 .... William Wells .... Tulane University
1966 .... William Wells .... Tulane University
1967 .... Richard Baumgarth .... Purdue University
1968 .... Marshall Boelter .... Univ. of Illinois, Chicago Circle Campus
1969 .... Nick Varner .... Purdue University
1970 .... Nick Varner .... Purdue University
1971 .... Keith Woestehoff .... Ohio University
1972 .... Andrew Tennent .... University of Wisconsin
1973 .... Dan Louie .... Washington State University
1974 .... Dan Louie .... Washington State University
1975 .... Robert Jewett .... University of California–Berkeley
1976 .... John Cianflone .... Rutgers University
1977 .... Jay Hungerford .... Arizona State University
1978 .... Steve Cusick .... University of Illinois–Urbana
1979 .... Peter Lhotka .... University of North Dakota
1980 .... Rob Havick .... University of Minnesota–Duluth
1981 .... (No Tournament)
1982 ....   Thomas Golly .... Penn State University
1983 .... Robert Madenjian .... Kansas State University
1984 .... Gary French .... California State College–Stanislaus
1985 .... (No Tournament)
1986 .... Gary Asbell .... Florida State University
1987 .... Bill Beardsley .... University of Michigan
1988 .... Nick Kucharew .... Mohawk College
1989 .... Gary Asbell .... Florida State University
1990 .... Marc Oelslager .... St. Cloud State University
1991 .... Frank Alonso .... University of Nebraska–Lincoln
1992 .... David Uwate .... University of Florida

ACU-I POCKET BILLIARD CHAMPIONS (Women)

1929 .... Margaret Anderson .... University of Illinois
1942 .... Emily Ann Julian .... South Dakota State College
1943 .... Mary Jean Noonan .... South Dakota State College
1944 .... Barbara Jackson .... Colorado State College of Ed.
1948 .... Jeanne Lynch .... Rhode Island State
1949 .... Cora Libbey .... University of Wisconsin
1950 .... (No Tournament)
1951 ....   Ramona Fielder .... South Dakota State College
1952 .... Sondra Bilsky .... Purdue University
1953 .... Joanne Skonning .... Purdue University
.... Jackie Slusher .... Oregon State College
1954 .... Lee McGary .... University of Oregon
1955 .... Judy Ferles .... University of Arizona

Year	Champion	University
1956	Judy Ferles	University of Arizona
1957	No Co-ed Face to Face	
1958	No Co-ed Face to Face	
1959	Jan Deeter	Purdue University
1960	Darlene McCabe	University of Oregon
1961	Ann Sidlauskas	Indiana University
1962	San Merrick	Bowling Green State University
1963	Barbara Watkins	Bowling Green State University
1964	Barbara Watkins	Bowling Green State University
1965	Susan Sloan	University of Texas
1966	Linda Randolph	Iowa State University
1967	Shirley Glicen	University of Miami
1968	Gail Allums	University of Iowa
1969	Donna Ries	University of Missouri at Kansas City
1970	Catherine Stephens	Western Washington State
1971	Marcia Girolamo	State Univ. of New York at Oswego
1972	Krista Hartmann	Santa Fe Junior College, Gainsville, Florida
1973	Marcia Girolamo	State University of New York at Oswego
1974	Janice Ogawa	Boise State University
1975	Debra Weiner	Northern Illinois University
1976	Melissa Rice	University of Wisconsin–Milwaukee
1977	Julie Bentz	University of Wisconsin–Madison
1978	Mari Dana Heydon	Oregon State University
1979	Julie Bentz Fitzpatrick	University of Wisconsin–Madison
1980	Shari Verrill	University of Wisconsin–Madison
1981	(No Tournament)	
1982	Jane Bartram	University of Colorado
1983	Helen Yamasaki	California State University–LA
1984	Shirley Weathers	Triton College
1985	(No Tournament)	
1986	Kathy Trabue	Ohio State University
1987	Penny Beile	University of Kentucky
1988	Janet Dordell	Penn State University
1989	Cathy Petrowski	North Texas State University
1990	Susan Tillotson	Florida State University
1991	Leanne Okada	University of California-Berkeley
1992	Laura Bendikas	University of Illinois-Urbana

1992 U.S. Open Champions
Loree Jon Jones and Mike Sigel

The site of the Roosevelt Hotel marked the first time the BCA U.S. Open had been held in New York City.   The event, sponsored by Brunswick Billiards and Blatt's Billiards, drew great crowds throughout the week and demonstrated a high interest in 14.1 Continuous still exists.

1992 BCA U.S. OPEN 14.1 CHAMPIONSHIPS
AUGUST 19-23 — Roosevelt Hotel / New York, NY
Final Ranking of Players - Men's Division

Rank	Name	Prize	Record	Balls Per Inning Average	High Run
1	Mike Sigel	$10,000	6-0	14.75	150
2	Dallas West	6,500	5-2	10.70	93
3	Mike Zuglan	4,000	5-2	9.73	148
4	Ray Martin	$2,500	4-2	14.55	109
5	Dick Lane	1,500	4-2	5.06	81
6	Jim Rempe	1,500	4-2	8.97	67
7	Johnny Archer	1,000	4-2	8.59	150
8	Steve Mizerak	1,000	3-2	9.25	134
9	Greg Fix	750	3-2	5.43	53
10	Allen Hopkins	750	3-2	7.92	88
11	Tony Robles	750	3-2	3.97	107
12	Nick Varner	750	2-2	5.72	88
13	Dan Barouty	450	2-2	5.16	65
14	Jim Fusco	450	2-2	3.74	64
15	Bob Hunter	450	2-2	7.47	57
16	Tom Karabatsos	450	2-2	7.81	59
17	Lou Butera		1-2	5.66	64
18	Jeff Carter		1-2	11.11	55
19	Ron Casanzio		1-2	5.49	56
20	Jack Colavita		1-2	2.88	34
21	Bill Dunsmore		1-2	5.02	40
22	John Ervoline		1-2	4.62	47
23	Grady Mathews		1-2	5.32	45
24	Oliver Ortmann		1-2	6.73	85
25	Pete Fusco		0-2	3.38	52
26	Keith Jones		0-2	3.51	33
27	Larry Lisciotti		0-2	4.88	38
28	Mike Massey		0-2	3.78	31
29	Cisero Murphy		0-2	1.50	16
30	Tom Ruocco		0-2	3.03	41
31	Mark Tadd		0-2	4.52	44
32	Bob Vanover		0-2	4.77	27

Tournment High Run-Mike Sigel, Johnny Archer (150)
Tournament Best Game-Mike Sigel (1 inning)

Final Ranking of Players - Women's Division

Rank	Name	Prize	Record	Balls Per Inning Average	High Run
1	Loree Jon Jones	$3,500	5-1	3.67	64
2	Ewa Mataya	2,300	4-1	4.02	68
3	Vivian Villarreal	1,800	4-2	3.34	25
4	Robin Bell	1,300	4-2	2.96	25
5	Billie Billing	750	2-2	2.17	25
6	Mary Kenniston	750	3-2	3.29	32
7	Belinda Bearden	300	2-2	1.69	32
8	Dawn Meurin	300	2-2	2.89	16
9	Peg Ledman		1-2	1.99	22
10	JoAnn Mason-Parker		1-2	1.97	21
11	Vicki Paski		1-2	2.44	13
12	Cathy Vanover		1-2	1.60	16
13	Nikki Benish		0-2	1.06	14
14	Fran Crini		0-2	1.82	18
15	Jeanette Lee		0-2	2.58	23
16	Nesli O'Hare		0-2	1.94	21

Tournment High Run-Ewa Mataya (68)
Tournament Best Game-Mary Kenniston (13 innings)

BCA'S U.S. OPEN 14.1 POCKET BILLIARD CHAMPIONSHIP RECORDS

Men's Division

Irving Crane 1966, Chicago, IL .... Runner-up–Joe Balsis
Jimmy Caras 1967, St. Louis, MO .... Runner-up–Luther Lassiter
Joe Balsis 1968, Lansing, MI .... Runner-up–Danny DiLiberto
Luther Lassiter 1969, Las Vegas, NV .... Runner-up–Jack Breit
Steve Mizerak 1970, Chicago, IL .... Runner-up–Luther Lassiter
Steve Mizerak 1971, Chicago, IL .... Runner-up–Joe Balsis
Steve Mizerak 1972, Chicago, IL .... Runner-up–Dan DiLiberto
Steve Mizerak 1973, Chicago, IL .... Runner-up–Luther Lassiter
Joe Balsis 1974, Chicago, IL .... Runner-up–Jim Rempe
Dallas West 1975, Chicago, IL .... Runner-up–Pete Margo
Tom Jennings 1976, Chicago, IL .... Runner-up–Joe Balsis
Tom Jennings 1977, Dayton, OH .... Runner-up–Richard Lane
Dallas West 1983, Detroit, MI .... Runner-up–Nick Varner
Oliver Ortmann 1989, Chicago, IL .... Runner-up–Steve Mizerak
Mike Sigel 1992, New York, NY .... Runner-up–Dallas West

Women's Division

Dorothy Wise 1967, St. Louis, MO .... Runner-up–San Lynn Merrick
Dorothy Wise 1968, Lansing, MI .... Runner-up–San Lynn Merrick
Dorothy Wise 1969, Las Vegas, NV .... Runner-up–San Lynn Merrick
Dorothy Wise 1970, Chicago, IL .... Runner-up–Shelia Bohm
Dorothy Wise 1971, Chicago, IL .... Runner-up–Geraldine Titcomb
Jean Balukas 1972, Chicago, IL .... Runner-up–Madelyn Whitlow
Jean Balukas 1973, Chicago, IL .... Runner-up–Donna Ries
Jean Balukas 1974, Chicago, IL .... Runner-up–Mieko Harada
Jean Balukas 1975, Chicago, IL .... Runner-up–Mieko Harada
Jean Balukas 1976, Chicago, IL .... Runner-up–Gloria Walker
Jean Balukas 1977, Dayton, OH .... Runner-up–Gloria Walker
Jean Balukas 1983, Detroit, MI .... Runner-up–Loree Jon Ogonowski
Loree Jon Jones 1989, Chicago, IL .... Runner-up–Robin Bell
Loree Jon Jones, 1992, New York, NY .... Runner-up–Ewa Mataya

U.S. OPEN RECORDS – 1966-1992
Men's Division

High run in the money: 150 by Irving Crane (vs. Joe Balsis), 1966/150 by Mike Sigel (vs. Jim Rempe), 1989/150 by Johnny Archer (vs. Jeff Carter), 1992; 150 by Mike Sigel (vs. Mike Zuglan), 1992.

High run out of the money: 116 by Rodney "Babe" Thompson, 1972.

High BPI average, career (minimum 3 Opens or 10 games): 12.47 by Steve Mizerak.

Most championships won: 4 by Steve Mizerak; (1970-1973 inclusive).

Most consecutive championships won: 4 by Steve Mizerak, (1970-1973 inclusive).

Most runner-up finishes: 3 by Balsis (1966, 1971, 1976) and Lassiter (1967, 1970, 1973).

Greatest victory margin (150-point match): 163 by Dick Baertsch (vs. Balsis), 1969.

Most games won, career: 55 by Joe Balsis (1966-1977 inclusive).

Best winning percentage, tournament: 1.000 by Crane, 1966; Mizerak, 1971; West, 1975; Sigel 1992.

Fewest innings by champion (32-man field): 53 by Steve Mizerak, 1972.

Most consecutive match victories: 12 by Steve Mizerak (1970-1972 inclusive).

Most high run awards: 3 by West (1966, 1967, 1976) and Balsis (1968, 1969, 1973).

Best game (150 points): 1 inning by Mike Sigel (vs. Mike Zuglan), 1992

Best game (200 points): 16 innings by Joe Balsis (vs. J. Rempe), 1974.

Most appearances, career: 15 by Dallas West (1966-1992 inclusive).

U.S. OPEN RECORDS – 1967-1992
Women's Division

High run in the money: 68 by Ewa Mataya (vs. Cathy Petrowski), 1992.

High run out of the money: 28 by Jean Ann (Williams) Cardwell, 1967.

High BPI average, tournament: 5.18 by Loree Jon Jones, 1989.

Most games, career: 58 by Gerry Titcomb.

Most innings, tournament (16-woman field): 373 by Madelyn Whitlow, 1972.

Most games won, career: 43 by Jean Balukas.

Best winning percentage, tournament: 1.000 by Wise (67-68, 70-71) and Balukas (72-83).

Best winning percentage, career (minimum 3 Opens or 10 games): .850 by Jean Balukas.

Most championships won: 7 by Jean Balukas; 1972-1983 inclusive.

Most consecutive championships won: 7 by Jean Balukas; 1972-1983 inclusive.

Most runner-up finishes: 2 by San Lynn Merrick, Gerry Titcomb and Mieko Harada.

Most third place finishes: 5 by Gerry Titcomb; 1970, 1972, 1974, 1975, 1976.

Most consecutive match victories: 37 by Jean Balukas (1972-1983 inclusive).

Most high run awards: 5 by Balukas (1972, 1973, 1975, 1977, 1983).

Best game (75 points): 3 innings by Jean Balukas (vs. Belinda Campos), 1977.

Best game (100 points): 13 innings by Loree Jon Jones (vs. Gerry Titcomb and vs. Belinda Bearden), 1989; by Robin Bell (vs. Gloria Walker), 1989; by Mary Kenniston (vs. Nesli O'Hare), 1992.

Best game (125 points): 13 innings by Loree Jon Jones (vs. Robin Bell), 1989.

Most appearances, career: 11 by Gerry Titcomb (1967-1989 inclusive).

MEN'S POCKET BILLIARD CHAMPIONS 1878-1990
Compiled by Charles Ursitti, Mike Shamos and Ken Shouler

The game of pocket billiards in the United States evolved slowly beginning in the 1830s. The present competitive form, known as straight pool or 14.1 continuous was not invented until 1910 and did not become the official championship game until 1912, when the term "pocket billiards" was first introduced. The earliest championship game was called "61-pool," a single-rack game with 15 numbered object balls. Each ball was worth a number of points equal to its numerical value; the first player to score at least 61 points was the winner. A match consisted of a race to a certain number of games, usually 21. This was the game played for the championship from 1878 until 1888.

Because a ball in 61-pool can be worth from 1 to 15 points, it was possible to win a match by sinking far fewer balls than one's opponent. This unfairness was corrected in 1889, when the game of "continuous pool" was introduced. The players still played individual fifteen-ball racks without a break ball, but each ball counted for only one point and the first player to reach a pre-determined point total, usually 100, was the winner. The player who sank the last ball of a rack would break the full pack on the next rack. No ball had to be called on the break, so it was possible for long runs to occur extending over many racks. The record run at continuous pool is still 96, achieved by Alfredo De Oro in a non-championship game in 1911.

The break shot in continuous pool was very risky, since it is difficult to sink a ball in a controlled fashion when hitting a full rack of fifteen balls. Top players tended to play safety at the end of a rack rather than miss with the balls spread. This caused title games to become boring, as the audience could look forward to an exchange of safeties every fifteen balls. To eliminate the problem, Jerome Keogh, the champion in 1910 and teacher of future champion Irving Crane, suggested that the last ball of each rack be left free to be used as a target on the next rack. He proposed the name, "14 racked, 1 ball free," which became 14.1 continuous. It was adopted as the championship form for the tournament of April, 1912, won by Edward Ralph, who thus became the first straight pool champion.

At first, championships were established by donors, such as the Brunswick-Balke-Collender Corporation. These expired after a certain time and a new tournament had to be held to determine the next champion. In between tournaments, the champion was obliged to defend the title against challengers, who would meet the champion in a two-man match. Until the 1940s, this was the dominant method by which the title was decided, much as in boxing. It is therefore incorrect in most cases to associate a single champion with a particular year. Not all tournaments advertised as "for the title" are listed, but only those that were sanctioned by an appropriate governing body.

The table below lists all 209 times that the pocket billiard title has changed hands or become vacant. The date listed is the month in which the title change occurred. (In some cases, tournaments or matches took place over a period of many months lasting as long as a baseball season.) The "Champion" is the name of the titleholder. "Runner-Up" indicates the player who lost the title match, or, in the case of a tournament, the player finishing in second place. From 1878 through 1888, the game was 61-pool. Continuous pool was the championship game from 1889 to 1911. Straight pool has been the championship game since 1912.

Date	Champion	Runner-Up
Apr, 1878	Cyrille Dion	Samuel F. Knight
Aug, 1878	Gotthard Walhstrom	Cyrille Dion
Apr, 1879	Samuel F. Knight	Gotthard Walhstrom
Aug, 1879	Alonzo Morris	Samuel F. Knight
Oct, 1879	Gotthard Walhstrom	Alonzo Morris
Feb, 1880	Samuel F. Knight	Gotthard Walhstrom
May 1880	Gotthard Walhstrom	Samuel F. Knight
Jan, 1881	Gotthard Walhstrom	Albert M. Frey
Jun, 1881	Gotthard Walhstrom	Albert M. Frey
Jan, 1884	James L. Malone	Albert M. Frey, Joseph T. King (tie)
Mar, 1886	Albert M. Frey	James L. Malone
May, 1886	Albert M. Frey	James L. Malone
Feb, 1887	Albert M. Frey	James L. Malone
Apr, 1887	Albert M. Frey	James L. Malone
May, 1887	James L. Malone	Albert M. Frey
May, 1887	Alfredo De Oro	James L. Malone
Feb, 1888	Alfredo De Oro	James L. Malone
Mar, 1889	Albert M. Frey	Alfredo De Oro
Apr, 1889	Title vacant (Frey died)	
Jun, 1889	Alfredo De Oro	Charles H. Manning
Apr, 1890	Alfredo De Oro	Charles H. Manning
May, 1890	Albert G. Powers	Alfredo De Oro
Jun, 1890	Charles H. Manning	Albert G. Powers
Aug, 1890	Charles H. Manning	George N. Kuntzsch
Oct, 1890	Charles H. Manning	Albert G. Powers
Jan, 1891	Albert G. Powers	Charles H. Manning
Mar, 1891	Albert G. Powers	P. H. Walsh
May, 1891	Alfredo De Oro	Albert G. Powers
Mar, 189	Alfredo De Oro	Albert G. Powers
Mar, 1893	Alfredo De Oro	Frank Sherman
Jun, 1893	Alfredo De Oro	P. H. Walsh
Dec, 1895	William Clearwater	Alfredo De Oro
Mar, 1896	William Clearwater	Jerome Keogh
Apr, 1896	William Clearwater	Alfredo De Oro
May, 1896	Alfredo De Oro	William Clearwater
Jun, 1896	Alfredo De Oro	Grant Eby
Fall, 1896	Herman E. Stewart	Alfredo De Oro
May, 1897	Grant Eby	Herman E. Stewart
Jun, 1897	Jerome Keogh	Grant Eby
Aug, 1897	Jerome Keogh	William Clearwater
Mar, 1898	William Clearwater	Jerome Keogh
Apr, 1898	Jerome Keogh	William Clearwater
Dec, 1898	Alfredo De Oro	Grant Eby, Frank Horgan (tie)
Jan, 1899	Alfredo De Oro	
Apr, 1899	Alfredo De Oro	Jerome Keogh
Dec, 1899	Alfredo De Oro	Fred Payton
Apr, 1900	Alfredo De Oro	Jerome Keogh
Mar, 1901	Frank Sherman	Alfredo De Oro
Apr, 1901	Alfredo De Oro	Frank Sherman
Mar, 1902	William Clearwater	Charles Weston
May, 1902	Grant Eby	William Clearwater
Dec, 1902	Grant Eby	P. H. Walsh
May, 1903	Title vacant	
Nov, 1904	Alfredo De Oro	Jerome Keogh
Nov, 1904	Alfredo De Oro	Jerome Keogh
Jan, 1905	Alfredo De Oro	Grant Eby
Mar, 1905	Jerome Keogh	Alfredo De Oro
May, 1905	Alfredo De Oro	Jerome Keogh
Oct, 1905	Alfredo De Oro	William Clearwater
Dec, 1905	Thomas Hueston	Alfredo De Oro
Feb, 1906	Thomas Hueston	Charles Weston
Apr, 1906	Thomas Hueston	Joe W. Carney
May, 1906	John Horgan	Thomas Hueston

Date	Champion	Runner-Up
Oct, 1906	John Horgan	Horace B. ("Jess") Lean
Oct, 1906	Jerome Keogh	John Horgan
Nov, 1906	Jerome Keogh	Fred Tallman
Dec, 1906	Thomas Hueston	Jerome Keogh
Feb, 190	Thomas Hueston	Edward Dawson
Apr, 1907	Thomas Hueston	Jerome Keogh
Apr, 1907	Thmas Hueston	William Clearwater
Jan, 1908	Thomas Hueston	Jerome Keogh
Jan, 1908	Title vacant	
Apr, 1908	Frank Sherman	Charles Weston
May, 1908	Alfredo De Oro	Frank Sherman
Oct, 1908	Alfredo De Oro	Bennie Allen
Nov, 1908	Thomas Hueston	Alfredo De Oro
Apr, 1909	Charles Weston	Thomas Hueston
May, 1909	Charles Weston	Horace B. ("Jess") Lean
Oct, 1909	John G. Kling	Charles Weston
Nov, 1909	Thomas Hueston	John G. Kling
Dec, 1909	Thomas Hueston	Bennie Allen
Feb, 1910	Jerome Keogh	Thomas Hueston
Mar, 1910	Jerome Keogh	Charles Weston
Apr, 1910	Jerome Keogh	Thomas Safford
Sep, 1910	Jerome Keogh	Thomas Hueston
Oct, 1910	Jerome Keogh	Bennie Allen
Nov, 1910	Alfredo De Oro	Jerome Keogh
Jan, 1911	Alfredo De Oro	William Clearwater
Mar, 1911	Alfredo De Oro	Thomas Hueston
Apr, 1911	Alfredo De Oro	Jerome Keogh
May, 1911	Alfredo De Oro	Charles Weston
Nov, 1911	Title vacant	
Apr, 1912	Edward Ralph	James Maturo
Jun, 1912	Alfredo De Oro	Edward Ralph
Nov, 1912	Alfredo De Oro	Frank Sherman
Jan, 1913	Alfredo De Oro	James Maturo
Feb, 1913	Alfredo De Oro	Thomas Hueston
Oct, 1913	Bennie Allen	Alfredo De Oro
Dec, 1913	Bennie Allen	Charles Weston
Jan, 1914	Bennie Allen	James Maturo
Apr, 1914	Bennie Allen	Edward Ralph
Jun, 1914	Bennie Allen	Ray R. Pratt
Dec, 1914	Bennie Allen	James Maturo
Dec, 1915	Title vacant	
Mar, 1916	W. Emmett Blankenship	Johnny Layton
May, 1916	Johnny Layton	W. Emmett Blankenship
Sep, 1916	Frank Taberski	Johnny Layton
Oct, 1916	Frank Taberski	Ralph Greenleaf
Nov, 1916	Frank Taberski	Edward Ralph
Jan, 1917	Frank Taberski	James Maturo
Feb, 1917	Frank Taberski	Louis Kreuter
Apr, 1917	Frank Taberski	Bennie Allen
May, 1917	Frank Taberski	Larry Stoutenberg
Oct, 1917	Frank Taberski	Joe Concannon
Nov, 1917	Frank Taberski	Louis Kreuter
Jan, 1918	Frank Taberski	Ralph Greenleaf
Jan, 1918	Title vacant	
Dec, 1919	Ralph Greenleaf	Bennie Allen
Nov, 1920	Ralph Greenleaf	Arthur Woods
Oct, 1921	Ralph Greenleaf	Arthur Woods
Dec, 1921	Ralph Greenleaf	Arthur Woods
Feb, 1922	Ralph Greenleaf	Thomas Hueston
May, 1922	Ralph Greenleaf	Walter Franklin
Oct, 1922	Ralph Greenleaf	Bennie Allen
Dec, 1922	Ralph Greenleaf	Arthur Church
Jan, 1923	Ralph Greenleaf	Thomas Hueston
Apr, 1924	Ralph Greenleaf	Bennie Allen

Date	Champion	Runner-Up
Apr, 1925	Frank Taberski	Ralph Greenleaf
Apr, 1926	Title vacant	
Nov, 1926	Ralph Greenleaf	Erwin Rudolph
Jan, 1927	Erwin Rudolph	Ralph Greenleaf
Mar, 1927	Erwin Rudolph	Harry Oswald
May, 1927	Thomas Hueston	Erwin Rudolph
Sep, 1927	Frank Taberski	Thomas Hueston
Nov, 1927	Frank Taberski	Pasquale Natalie
Jan, 1928	Frank Taberski	Arthur Woods
Mar, 1928	Ralph Greenleaf	Frank Taberski
May, 1928	Ralph Greenleaf	Andrew St. Jean
Dec, 1928	Frank Taberski	Ralph Greenleaf
Dec, 1929	Ralph Greenleaf	Erwin Rudolph
Dec, 1930	Erwin Rudolph	Ralph Greenleaf
Dec, 1931	Ralph Greenleaf	George Kelly
Dec, 1932	Ralph Greenleaf	Jimmy Caras
May, 1933	Ralph Greenleaf	Andrew Ponzi
Dec, 1933	Erwin Rudolph	Andrew Ponzi
Feb, 1934	Andrew Ponzi	Erwin Rudolph
1934	Title vacant	
Dec, 1935	Jimmy Caras	Erwin Rudolph
Apr, 1936	Jimmy Caras	Erwin Rudolph
Apr, 1937	Ralph Greenleaf	Andrew Ponzi
Nov, 1937	Ralph Greenleaf	Irving Crane
Dec, 1937	Ralph Greenleaf	Irving Crane
Mar, 1938	Jimmy Caras	Andrew Ponzi
Apr, 1938	Jimmy Caras	Andrew Ponzi
Apr, 1940	Andrew Ponzi	Jimmy Caras
May, 1941	Willie Mosconi	Andrew Ponzi
Nov, 1941	Erwin Rudolph	Irving Crane
May, 1942	Irving Crane	Erwin Rudolph
Dec, 1942	Willie Mosconi	Andrew Ponzi
Apr, 1943	Andrew Ponzi	Willie Mosconi
Dec, 1943	Andrew Ponzi	Irving Crane
Mar, 1944	Willie Mosconi	Andrew Ponzi
Feb, 1945	Willie Mosconi	Ralph Greenleaf
Mar, 1946	Willie Mosconi	Jimmy Caras
Nov, 1946	Willie Mosconi	Irving Crane
Dec, 1946	Irving Crane	Willie Mosconi
May, 1947	Willie Mosconi	Irving Crane
Nov, 1947	Willie Mosconi	Jimmy Caras
Mar, 1948	Willie Mosconi	Andrew Ponzi
Feb, 1949	Jimmy Caras	Willie Mosconi
Feb, 1950	Willie Mosconi	Irving Crane
Jan, 1951	Willie Mosconi	Irving Crane
Feb, 1951	Willie Mosconi	Irving Crane
Apr, 1952	Willie Mosconi	Irving Crane
Mar, 1953	Willie Mosconi	Joe Procita
Mar, 1955	Willie Mosconi	Joe Procita
Apr, 1955	Irving Crane	Willie Mosconi
Dec, 1955	Willie Mosconi	Irving Crane
Feb, 1956	Willie Mosconi	Jimmy Caras
Mar, 1956	Willie Mosconi	Jimmy Moore
Apr, 1956	Willie Mosconi	Irving Crane
Apr, 1963	Luther Lassiter	Jimmy Moore
Aug, 1963	Luther Lassiter	Jimmy Moore
Mar, 1964	Luther Lassiter	Arthur Cranfield
Sep, 1964	Arthur Cranfield	Luther Lassiter
Mar, 1965	Joe Balsis	Jimmy Moore
Mar, 1965	Joe Balsis	Jimmy Moore
Mar, 1966	Luther Lassiter	Cisero Murphy
Dec, 1966	Luther Lassiter	Cisero Murphy
Apr, 1967	Luther Lassiter	Jack Breit
Dec, 1967	Luther Lassiter	Jack Breit

Date	Champion	Runner-Up
Apr, 1968	Irving Crane	Luther Lassiter
Feb, 1969	Ed Kelly	Cisero Murphy
Feb, 1970	Irving Crane	Steve Mizerak
Feb, 1971	Ray Martin	Joe Balsis
Feb, 1972	Irving Crane	Lou Butera
Feb, 1973	Lou Butera	Irving Crane
Feb, 1974	Ray Martin	Allen Hopkins
Aug, 1976	Larry Lisciotti	Steve Mizerak
Aug, 1977	Allen Hopkins	Pete Margo
Aug, 1978	Ray Martin	Allen Hopkins
Aug, 1979	Mike Sigel	Joe Balsis
Aug, 1980	Nick Varner	Mike Sigel
Aug, 1981	Mike Sigel	Nick Varner
Aug, 1982	Steve Mizerak	Danny DiLiberto
Aug, 1983	Steve Mizerak	Jimmy Fusco
Aug, 1985	Mike Sigel	Jim Rempe
Aug, 1986	Nick Varner	Allen Hopkins
Jan, 1990	Bobby Hunter	Ray Martin

WOMEN'S POCKET BILLIARD CHAMPIONSHIPS
WORLD 14.1 CHAMPIONSHIPS

Date	Champion	Runner-Up
Feb, 1974	Meiko Harada	Jean Balukas
Aug, 1977	Jean Balukas	Gloria Walker
Aug, 1978	Jean Balukas	Billie Billing
Dec, 1979	Jean Balukas	Mary Kenniston (WPBA Nat'ls)
Aug, 1980	Jean Balukas	Billie Billing
Aug, 1981	Loree Jon Ogonowski	Vicki Frechen
Aug, 1982	Jean Balukas	Loree Jon Ogonowski
Aug, 1983	Jean Balukas	Loree Jon Ogonowski
Aug, 1985	Belinda Bearden	Mary Kenniston
Aug, 1986	Loree Jon Jones	Mary Kenniston

WPBA NATIONAL CHAMPIONS

Date	Champion	Runner-Up
1978	Jean Balukas	Billie Billing (14.1)
1979	Jean Balukas	Mary Kenniston (14.1)
1980	Gloria Walker	Sabra MacArthur (Nine Ball)
1983	Jean Balukas	Belinda Bearden (Nine Ball)
1984	Jean Balukas	Mary Kenniston (Nine Ball)
1985	Belinda Bearden	Linda Haywood (Nine Ball)
1986	Jean Balukas	Mary Kenniston (Nine Ball)
1987	Mary Kenniston	Loree Jon Jones (Nine Ball)
1988	Loree Jon Jones	Robin Bell (Nine Ball)
1989	Robin Bell	Loree Jon Jones (Nine Ball)
1990	Loree Jon Jones	Ewa Mataya (Nine Ball)
1991	Ewa Mataya	Belinda Bearden (Nine Ball)
1992	Vivian Villarreal	Ewa Mataya (Nine Ball)

WORLD POOL BILLIARD ASSN. WORLD NINE BALL CHAMPIONS

Men

Date	Champion	Runner-Up
1990	Earl Strickland (USA)	Jeff Carter (USA)
1991	Earl Strickland (USA)	Nick Varner (USA)
1992	Johnny Archer (USA)	Bobby Hunter (USA)

Women

Date	Champion	Runner-Up
1990	Robin Bell (USA)	Loree Jon Jones (USA)
1991	Robin Bell (USA)	Joann Mason (USA)
1992	Franzistva Stark (Germany)	Vivian Villarreal (USA)

Junior

Date	Champion	Runner-Up
1992	Hui-Kai Hsia (Taiwan)	Michael Coltrain (USA)

1992 WPA World Nine-Ball Championships: (Juniors, Kneeling L-R) Ming-Te Tsou (3rd-Taiwan), Lasse Alyesalo (3rd-Finland), Michael Coltrain (2nd-USA), Hui-Kai Hsia (World Champion-Taiwan);   (Women, 2nd Row, L-R) Robin Bell (3rd-USA), Peg Ledman (3rd-USA), Franziska Stark (World Champion-Germany), Vivian Villarreal (2nd-USA),   (Men, top row, L-R) Kim Davenport (3rd-USA), Efren Reyes (3rd-Philippines), Johnny Archer (World Champion-USA), Bob Hunter (2nd-USA).

PRO TOUR CHAMPIONS—1991-1992

PROFESSIONAL BILLIARD TOUR ASSOCIATION SANCTIONED:
1991-Bicycle Club Invitational-Buddy Hall
Sands Nine-Ball Open XIV-Jim Rempe
1992-5th Annual Rakm Up Classic-Buddy Hall
Los Angeles Open-Earl Strickland
International Eight-Ball Classic-Efren Reyes
International Nine-Ball Classic-Johnny Archer
Sands Nine-Ball Open XV-Johnny Archer
Bicycle Club Invitational II-Mike Sigel
16th Annual US Open 14.1-Mike Sigel
17th Annual US Open Nine-Ball-Tommy Kennedy
PBTA National Championship-Roger Griffis
Sands Nine-Ball Open XVI-Earl Strickland

WOMEN'S PROFESSIONAL BILLIARD ASSOCIATION SANCTIONED:
1991-Big Island Classic-Robin Bell
Wahine Classic-Vivian Villarreal
WPBA Nationals-Ewa Mataya
1992-Los Angeles Open-Peg Ledman
International Nine-Ball Classic-Vivian Villarreal
16th Annual US Open 14.1-Loree Jon Jones
17th Annual US Open Nine-Ball-Robin Bell
WPBA Nationals-Vivian Villarreal

FINAL 1992 RANKINGS:

1.	Buddy Hall	1175 Pts
2.	Johnny Archer	1095
3.	Earl Strickland	815
4.	Mile Sigel	750
5.	Nick Varner	730
6.	Jim Rempe	710
7.	C.J. Wiley	670
8.	Steve Mizerak	665
9.	Kim Davenport	660
10.	Jose Parca	570
11.	David Howard	550
12.	Roger Griffis	535
13.	Mike Lebron	480
14.	Dennis Hatch	445
15.	Ernesto Dominguez	400
16.	Tony Ellin	395

FINAL 1992 RANKINGS:

1.	Ewa Mataya	1215 Pts
2.	Robin Bell	1145
3.	Vivian Villarreal	1035
4.	JoAnn Mason-Parker	830
5.	Peg Ledman	745
6.	Belinda Bearden	700
7.	Tammie Wesley	670
8.	Mary Kenniston	555
9.	Loree Jon Jones	555
10.	Kelly Oyama	495
11.	Nikki Benish	490
12.	Laura Smith	485
13.	Franziska Stark	445
14.	Billie Billing	360
15.	Michelle Adams	355
16	Yohko Okumura	335

NATIONAL CHAMPIONS — BILLIARD FEDERATION OF U.S.A.

1968	Allen Gilbert	1979	Eddie Robin
1969	Bill Hynes	1980	Harry Sims
1970	Allen Gilbert	1981	George Ashby
1971	Allen Gilbert	1982	Carlos Hallon
1972	Eddie Robin	1983	Harry Sims
1973	John Bonner	1984	George Ashby
1974	Frank Torres	1985	Frank Torres
1975	John Bonner	1986	Carlos Hallon
1976	George Ashby	1987	Allen Gilbert
1977	Allen Gilbert	1988	Allen Gilbert
1978	Frank Torres		

NATIONAL CHAMPIONS — AMERICAN BILLIARDS ASSOCIATION

1969	Bud Harris
1970	Bud Harris
1971	Jim Cattrano
1972	Jim Cattrano
1973	Allen Gilbert
1974	not held
1975	George Ashby
1976	Allen Gilbert
1977	Allen Gilbert
1978	George Ashby
1979	George Ashby
1980	George Ashby

Regional Tournaments only were held in 1981-1988

1981	Carlos Hallon	Eastern
	George Ashby	Central
	Allen Gilbert	Western
1982	Chris Bartzos	Eastern
	Bill Hawkins	Central
	Allen Gilbert	Western
1983	Dick Reid	Eastern
	George Ashby	Central
	Allen Gilbert	Western

1984	Carlos Hallon	Eastern
	George Ashby	Central
	not held	Western
1985	3 tied for 1st	Eastern
	Ira Goldberg	
	Bill Maloney	
	Dick Reid	
	George Ashby	Central
	Rick Bryck	Western
1986	Dick Reid	Eastern
	Bill Smith	Central
	Nahib Yousri	Western
1987	Dick Reid	Eastern
	George Ashby	Central
	Harry Sims	Western
1988	Carols Hallon	Eastern
	Mike Donnelly	Central
	Allen Gilbert	Western

In September 1988, the BFUSA and ABA merged to form The United States Billiard Association.

NATIONAL CHAMPIONS — U.S. BILLIARD ASSOCIATION

1989	Carlos Hallon (grand average: 1.104)
1990	Sang Chun Lee (grand average: 1.471)
1991	Sang Chun Lee (grand average: 1.464)
1992	Sang Chun Lee (grand average: 1.591)

WORLD THREE CUSHION CHAMPIONS (Professional)
[Sanctioned tournaments held in the United States.]

1878	Leon Magnus	1910	Fred Eames
1899	W. H. Catton	1910	Thomas Hueston
1900	Eugene Carter	1910	Alfredo De Oro
1900	Lloyd Jevne	1910	John W. Daly
1907	Harry P. Cline	1911	Alfredo De Oro
1908	John W. Daly	1912	Joseph W. Carney
1908	Thomas Hueston	1912	John Horgan
1908	Alfredo De Oro	1913-14	Alfredo De Oro
1909	Alfredo De Oro	1915	George Moore

1915	William H. Huey
1915	Alfredo De Oro
1916	Charles Ellis
1916	Charles McCourt
1916	Hugh Heal
1916	George Moore
1917	Charles McCourt
1917	Robert L. Cannefax
1917	Alfredo De Oro
1918	Augie Kieckhefer
1919	Alfredo De Oro
1919	Robert L. Cannefax
1920	John Layton
1921	Augie Kieckhefer
1921-22	John Layton
1923	Tiff Denton
1924-25	Robert L. Cannefax
1926	Otto Reiselt
1927	Augie Kieckhefer
1927	Otto Reiselt
1928-30	John Layton
1931	Arthur Thurnblad
1932	Augie Kieckhefer
1933	Welker Cochran
1934	John Layton
1935	Welker Cochran
1936	William Hoppe
1936-37	Welker Cochran
1938	Roger Conti*
1939	Joseph Chamaco
1940-43	William F. Hoppe
1944-46	Welker Cochran
1947-52	William F. Hoppe
1953	Raymond Kilgore
1954	Harold Worst
1964	Arthur Rubin
1969	Juan Navarra
1972	Juan Navarra
1984	Ludo Dielis
1988	Ludo Dielis
1989	Torbjorn Blomdahl
1990	Raymond Ceulemans
1991	Torbjorn Blomdahl
1992	Torbjorn Blomdahl

* Tournament held in Paris, France, with Welker Cochran and Jake Schaefer in the field.

WORLD THREE CUSHION CHAMPIONS (Amateur)

1928-29	Edmond Soussa, Egypt
1930	H. J. Robyns, Holland
1931	Enrique Miro, Spain
1932-33	H. J. Robyns, Holland
1934	Claudio Puigvert, Spain
1935	Alfredo Lagache, France
1936	Edward L. Lee, U.S.A.
1937	Alfredo Lagache, France
1938	Augusto Vergez, Argentina
1948	Rene Vingerhoedt, Belgium
1952	Pedro L. Carrera, Argentina
1953 & 58	Enrique Navarra, Argentina
1960	Rene Vingerhoedt, Belgium
1961	Adolfo Suarez, Peru
1963-73	Raymond Ceulemans, Belgium
1974	Nobuaki Kobayashi, Japan
1975-80	Raymond Ceulemans, Belgium
1981	Ludo Dielis, Belgium
1982	Rini Van Bracht, Holland
1983	Raymond Ceulemans, Belgium
1984	Nabuaki Kobayashi, Japan
1985	Raymond Ceulemans, Belgium
1986	Avelino Rico, Spain
1987	Torbjorn Blomdahl, Sweden

* World amateur tournament discontinued.

World Cup Three Cushion Champions (Professional)
[Champion determined by results of four to seven tournaments. Matches are best 3 out of 5 fifteen-point games. Single elimination format.]

1986	Raymond Ceulemans, Belgium
1987	Raymond Ceulemans, Belgium
1988	Torbjorn Blomdahl, Sweden
1989	Ludo Oielis, Belgium
1990	Raymond Ceulemans, Belgium
1991	Torbjorn Blomdahl, Sweden
1992	Torbjorn Blomdahl, Sweden

Three Cushion Records
[Classic era (before 1960) - Ivory balls]

Best tournament grand average:	Willie Hoppe, 1950, 1.333
Best league game:	50 pts. in 16 innings, Otto Reiselt, 1926
Best tournament game:	50 pts. in 23 innings, Jay Bozeman, 1940, 1952
High Run, exhibition:	25, Willie Hoppe, 1918
High run, league:	20, Willie Hoppe, 1928
	18, John Layton, 1926
	18, Joe Chamaco, 1939
High run, tournament:	18, Charles Morin, 1915
	17, Gus Copulus, 1930
	17, Tiff Denton, 1940
High run, match:	20, Willie Hoppe, 1945
High run, practice games:	22, Gus Copulos, Welker Cochran

[Modern era (after 1960) - Cast phenolic balls]

Best tournament grand average:	2.204, Blomdahl, Tokyo, Japan, 1992
	1.745, Ceulemans, Las Vegas, Nevada, 1986
	1.679, Ceulemans, Las Vegas, Nevada, 1978
	1.541, Ceulemans, H-Ointher, Holland, 1985
	1.447, Ceulemans, Aix-les-Baines, France, 1983
Best tournament games:	50 pts. in 16 innings, Sang Lee (vs. Torbjorn Blomdahl), 1992
High run, tournament:	26, Raymond Ceulemans in Simonis Cup, 1968
High run, inter-club match:	23, Raymond Ceulemans, 1969
High run, USA regional tournament:	19, Bill Hawkins, 1977
High run, exhibition:	22, Torbjorn Blomdahl (vs. Sung Lee), 1992

High runs, not scored in major tournament or exhibitions:

	32, Raymond Ceulemans (Belgium)
	31, Yoshio Yoshihara (Japan)
	24, Torbjorn Blomdahl (Sweden)
	22, Allen Gilbert (USA)

UNITED STATES SNOOKER ASSOCIATION NATIONAL CHAMPIONSHIP

1991 .... Tom Kollins   1992 .... Tom Kollins

WORLD PROFESSIONAL BILLIARD AND SNOOKER ASSOCIATION WORLD CHAMPIONSHIP

1927-40	Joe Davis	1958-63	Not held
1941-45	Not held	1964	John Pulman
1946	Joe Davis	1965	John Pulman
1947	Walter Donaldson	1966	John Pulman
1948	Fred Davis	1967	Not held
1949	Fred Davis	1968	John Pulman
1950	Walter Donaldson	1969	John Spencer
1951	Fred Davis	1970	Ray Spencer
1952	Fred Davis	1971	(Played in Nov. 1970) John Spencer
1953	Fred Davis	1971	Not held
1954	Fred Davis	1972	Alex Higgins
1955	Fred Davis	1973	Ray Reardon
1956	Fred Davis	1974	Ray Reardon
1957	John Pulman	1975	Ray Reardon

1976	Ray Reardon
1977	John Spencer
1978	Ray Reardon
1979	Terry Griffiths
1980	Cliff Thorburn
1981	Steve Davis
1982	Alex Higgins
1983	Steve Davis
1984	Steve Davis

1985	Dennis Taylor
1986	Joe Johnson
1987	Steve Davis
1988	Steve Davis
1989	Steve Davis
1990	Stephen Hendry
1991	John Parrot
1992	Stephen Hendry

WORLD LADIES BILLIARD AND SNOOKER ASSOCIATION WORLD CHAMPIONSHIP

1976	Vera Selby
1977	Not held
1978	Not held
1979	Not held
1980	Lesley McIlrath
1981	Vera Selby
1982	Not held
1983	Sue Foster
1984	Not held

1985	Allison Fisher
1986	Allison Fisher
1987	Ann-Marie Farren
1988	Allison Fisher
1989	Allison Fisher
1990	Karen Corr
1991	Allison Fisher
1992	Not held

BCA Sanctioning Of Billiard Tournaments

BCA offers tournament sanctioning for amateur and professional tournaments for a nominal fee. This official sanction signifies the tournament's authenticity.

With each sanction, the sponsor shall receive the following:

- Official Rules & Record Book
- Double Elimination pairing charts
- Official Tournament Report Forms
- Official Tournament Sanction Certificate
- BCA Logo Sheet
- Advance listing in the BCA BREAK newsletter
- Recognition of the tournament and winner in the next BCA Official Rules and Record Book

Please send us a Sanction Application for:

(type of tournament) _____

Name _____

Company _____

Address_____

City _____ State _____ Zip _____

Home Phone _____ Business Phone _____

Return to: BCA, 1700 S. 1st Avenue, Iowa City, IA 52240

Searching for something to improve your game... look no more!

Become a BCA sanctioned player member.

- As a sanctioned player member you will be eligible to participate in the annual BCA National Individual & Team Tournaments. Over $200,000 in cash and prizes are awarded each year.

- When you join BCA as a sanctioned player member, you will receive complimentary copies of the Official Rules & Records Book and the "How to Play Pool Right" instructional booklet.

- In addition, you will also receive member discounts, the BREAK newsletter and much, much more. And all this for only $25.

☐ *YES, I want to reap the benefits of BCA membership. Enroll me as a member today. My check for $25 is enclosed.*

☐ *YES, I am interested in joining BCA. Please send me additional information.*

Name _____

Address _____

City _____ State _____ Zip _____

Date _____ Phone __ _____

Return to: BCA, 1700 S. 1st Avenue, Iowa City, IA 52240

Together,
We can make billiards the sport of the '90s.

By becoming a member of BCA, you will become part of the industry-wide movement to promote pool and billiards.

Manufacturer, Distributor, Importer Member $1000
    (Represented by 12 members on the board)
Associate Member (has $1/2$ vote) 500
Retail Member 250
Proprietor Member
    8 + tables 100
    1-7 tables 50
Coin Machine Operator 100

☐ *YES, I would like to become a member of BCA.*

Name _____

Company Name _____

Address _____

City _____ State _____ Zip _____

Date _____ Phone _____

Signature _____

☐ My check for $ _____ is enclosed.

Return to: BCA, 1700 S. 1st Avenue, Iowa City, IA 52240

NOTES

BCA PRESIDENTS AND VICE-PRESIDENTS

YEAR	PRESIDENT	VICE-PRESIDENT
1966	William Gunklach	Nat Wexler
1967	Bud Hobbs	James F. Wilhem
1968	William Gunklach	James F. Wilhem
1969	James F. Wilhem	Norman Altholf
1970	James F. Wilhem	Norman Altholf
1971	James F. Wilhem	Norman Altholf
1972	Charles L. Bailey	Robert Weise
1973	Charles L. Bailey	Thomas B. Marsh
1974	Michael Geiger	Thomas B. Marsh
1975	Michael Geiger	Thomas B. Marsh
1976	Kim Gandy	Clint Fleming
1977	Kim Gandy	Clint Fleming
1978	Paul Lucchesi	James F. Wilhem
1979	Darrell Lawless	James F. Wilhem
1980	James F. Wilhem	Don Canfield
1981	James F. Wilhem	Don Canfield
1982	Paul Huebler	Conrad Burkman
1983	Paul Huebler	Conrad Burkman
1984	Paul Huebler	Conrad Burkman
1985	David Maidment	Charles Robertson
1986	Charles Robertson	Jerry Briesath
1987	Charles Robertson	Jerry Briesath
1988	Charles Robertson	Jerry Briesath
1989	James Bakula	Jerry Briesath
1990	James Bakula	Jerry Briesath
1991	David Maidment	Daniel Gauci
1992	Daniel Gauci	Raoul Rubalcava